ACADEMIC
Listening
ENCOUNTERS
Listening, Note Taking, and Discussion

Teacher's Manual

CONTENT
FOCUS
Human Behavior

MIRIAM ESPESETH

CAMBRIDGE
UNIVERSITY PRESS

CAMBRIDGE UNIVERSITY PRESS
Cambridge, New York, Melbourne, Madrid, Cape Town, Singapore, São Paulo

Cambridge University Press
32 Avenue of the Americas, New York, NY 10013–2473, USA

www.cambridge.org
Information on this title: www.cambridge.org/9780521578202

First published 1999
4th printing 2006

Printed in the United States of America

A catalog record for this publication is available from the British Library

Library of Congress Cataloging in Publication Data
Espeseth, Miriam.
Academic listening encounters : listening, note taking, and discussion :
content focus, human behavior / Miriam Espeseth.
p. cm.
ISBN-13 978-0-521-57820-2 Teacher's Manual
ISBN-10 0-521-57820-5 Teacher's Manual
1. English language – Textbooks for foreign speakers. 2. Study skills – Problems,
exercises, etc. 3. Listening – Problems, exercises, etc. I. Title.
PE1128.E83   1998
428.2′4 – dc21

98-21469
CIP

ISBN-13 978-0-521-57820-2 Teacher's Manual
ISBN-10 0-521-57820-5 Teacher's Manual

Book design by Jill Little, *Mediamark*
Text Composition by *American Composition & Graphics, Inc.*

Contents

Introduction

This introduction provides an overview of the goals and contents of *Academic Listening Encounters*, as well as general teaching suggestions and guidelines for its use in the classroom.

Specific chapter-by-chapter suggestions follow in the next section, beginning on page 3. That section also contains the answer key for the tasks in the Student's Book.

The third section of this book, the Listening Script, contains a complete transcript of the material on the *Academic Listening Encounters* audiotape, and the last section provides quizzes on the lectures.

OVERVIEW

Academic Listening Encounters is a content-based listening skills course designed primarily for academic-bound students of English, but also suitable for any learners of English who want to improve their general listening skills. The primary goal of the course is to prepare students for success in academic and also everyday settings. To this end, the listening materials include several types of spoken English: (1) general informational material, which students use to perform specific tasks; (2) conversations (in the form of interviews); and (3) academic lectures. These three types of discourse appear in each of the book's ten chapters. Working through the chapters, students do a wide variety of listening tasks, including listening for specific ideas, following directions, and completing summaries and outlines. The book puts a major focus on helping students learn note taking – an essential academic skill.

Another skill actively promoted in this course is oral fluency, and for this reason there is a great deal of pair and small group work, as well as many opportunities for students to give oral presentations to the class. The In Your Own Voice section in each chapter encourages students to respond to chapter topics personally or to analyze issues related to the topic, through discussions with classmates, oral presentations, and surveys. Throughout the book, critical thinking skills important for academic success, such as making inferences and synthesizing information, are highlighted.

A secondary goal of the course is to present cultural content about the United States, with a view to promoting class discussion of cultural differences and universals. ESL/EFL students are a tremendous source of cultural information, and this course exploits that source.

The content focus of the book is *human behavior*. The specific topics covered within the ten chapters were chosen for their universal appeal, and they should be of relevance and concern to your students. They include such diverse issues as the effects of stress on the body, problems of adolescence, body language across cultures, and why people are attracted to each other. The ten chapter topics are grouped into five general topics, corresponding to the book's five units, each of which contains two chapters. For example, the general topic of Unit Two is *"development through life."* Its two chapters focus on issues and problems relating to adolescence and early adulthood, respectively.

The listening material for each chapter includes an unscripted conversation or informal interview with one or more real-life individuals that explores a particular aspect of the chapter topic. In addition, each chapter contains an authentic mini-lecture given by a professor or other expert presenting content that students might encounter in an introductory social science course.

CHAPTER ORGANIZATION

CHAPTER OUTLINE

Each chapter of *Academic Listening Encounters* is structured to maximize students' understanding of the chapter topic. Vocabulary and ideas recycle through the four sections of each chapter, and recur in later chapters, as students move from listening to discussing, and from informal to academic discourse.

Here is a brief description of the organization of the chapters in *Academic Listening Encounters*. Additional information can be found under Chapter Format and Teaching Suggestions in the Introduction to the Student's Book.

1 Getting Started

This section contains a short reading task and a listening task. The reading task is designed to activate students' prior knowledge about the topic and to generate students' interest. Students answer comprehension questions on the reading and discuss the issues they raise.

The listening task in this section may require students to complete a graph, listen for specific information, do a matching exercise, or do something physical. This task provides skill-building practice and gives students a listening warm-up on the chapter topic.

2 American Voices

This section contains one or more informal interviews on issues related to the chapter topic. It is divided into three subsections:

Before the Interview

This subsection contains a prelistening task that calls on students either to predict the content of the interview or to share what they already know about the topic from their personal or cultural experience. (Be sure to take enough time with this task for all students to contribute.)

Interviews

In this subsection students listen to the interviews. The interviews are divided into two or three parts both on the audiotape and in the Student's Book to facilitate comprehension.

Each interview segment begins with a vocabulary preview: a bordered box glossing words and phrases from the interview that students may not know. These words and phrases are given in the context in which students will hear them and are followed by definitions.

After each vocabulary preview, students read either a list of questions they will be asked to answer or a partially completed summary of the interview they are about to hear. Then they listen to the audiotaped interview segment. After listening, they answer the questions or complete the summary. This approach allows students to demonstrate their understanding of the tape, provides a framework for listening, and teaches basic listening skills.

After the Interview

In this subsection students are given the opportunity to explore the topic more deeply through additional reading, sharing their own perspectives, drawing inferences, or thinking critically about what they have heard. Most of the tasks in this section are for pairs or small groups.

3 In Your Own Voice

The tasks in this section are designed to give students a chance to take creative control of the topic. Specific tasks are determined by the chapter content. The following tasks are included in some form in nearly every chapter:

- Sharing your personal perspective: Students talk with partners or in small groups, sharing their own experiences or opinions.
- Gathering data: Students gather data by questioning one or more people, either classmates or people outside the class. This step may be done in class, as homework, or by visiting another class if one is available. If students are writing their own interview or survey questions, check their questions before they begin to gather data.
- Presenting data: Students prepare and present their data in an informal speech. Stress that this is a "practice" situation, a chance for students to get comfortable speaking to an audience in English.

4 Academic Listening and Note Taking

This section contains an authentic audiotaped lecture on an aspect of the chapter topic. This section is divided into three subsections:

Before the Lecture

The first task of this subsection calls on students to predict the content of the lecture, to explore what they already know about the topic, or to do a brief reading exercise designed to provide them with background information they will need to understand the lecture content.

Following this first task is the presentation and practice of an academic note-taking skill; the specific nature of the skill is determined by the particular structure or language of the lecture. The skill is explained in a shaded task commentary box, and after reading the box students do a listening task designed to practice it. The audiotaped material used in this listening task is drawn from the lecture itself.

Lecture

In this subsection students hear the lecture. To facilitate student comprehension, all lectures are divided into two parts, both on the audiotape and in the Student's Book.

Each lecture part is preceded by a matching or multiple-choice vocabulary task designed to introduce vocabulary that students will encounter in the lecture and help them develop their ability to guess meaning from context. The words and phrases are given in the context in which they will be heard in the lecture.

Following the vocabulary task, students preview a comprehension task for the lecture. The task may involve completing a partial summary or an outline, or answering comprehension questions. The task generally reinforces the note-taking skill taught in Before the Lecture. Students are instructed to take notes during each part of the lecture, and then to use their notes to complete the lecture comprehension task.

After the Lecture

This subsection includes one or both of the following task types:

- Analyzing additional information: Tasks of this type allow students to deepen their understanding of the chapter topic, often by synthesizing information from the lecture and the American Voices section. Additional information related to the chapter topic is often presented to students in the form of a paragraph or statistics.
- Sharing personal/cultural perspectives: Discussion questions lead students to think critically about the chapter content and to present their own views.

SPECIAL FEATURES

Task Commentary Boxes

Throughout the book, the title of each task describes the skill that it practices. When a task type appears for the first time, it is followed by a shaded commentary box. The material in the box explains to the student why that particular skill is important and how to practice it. Through this feature, students can learn to apply the skills and approaches to listening learned and practiced in this book to other contexts. At the back of the Student's Book, there is an alphabetized index of all the tasks.

Note-taking Skills

Section 4 of each chapter, Academic Listening and Note Taking, presents a specific academic note-taking skill; the presentation includes a boxed explanation of the skill, followed by a taped task providing practice with the skill. The ten note-taking tasks presented in this course were chosen to help students develop the skills they will need to be successful note takers in an academic lecture course. These include such skills as using symbols and abbreviations; using space to show organizational structure; and paying attention to signal words. Go over the information in the task commentary box carefully with students before you begin each note-taking task. In the steps that follow, students listen to segments of the lecture that they are about to hear, and practice a note-taking skill.

Audiotape

The audiotape contains the conversations, interviews, and lectures for the course, as well as the material for the listening warm-ups in Section 1 (Getting Started) of each chapter. It also contains the listening material for note-taking tasks in Section 4. Tasks for which there is accompanying audiotaped material are marked in the Student's Book with 🎧. The specific location (or step) where students should listen to the tape is marked with a cassette symbol.

The interviewees in *Academic Listening Encounters* include both native and non-native speakers of English. The lectures are authentic, prepared, and given by professors or other experts.

Note that the material on tape is provided in printed form in this manual, in the section titled Listening Script.

SCHEDULING THE COURSE

Each chapter of *Academic Listening Encounters* represents approximately 7 to 11 hours of classroom material. Thus, with a 90-minute daily class, a teacher could complete all ten chapters in a ten-week course. For use with a shorter course, a teacher could certainly omit chapters or activities within chapters. The course could also be expanded with the use of guest speakers, debates, movies, and other authentic audiotaped material. See the specific suggestions below for skipping or adding material.

The following chart gives approximate class times for each of the sections and subsections in a chapter. Of course, times may vary according to the needs and interests of your class.

Section	Approximate Class Time
1 Getting Started	1 hour

2 American Voices
    Before the Interview
    Interview
    After the Interview
	
	½ hour
	1–2 hours
	½–1 hour

3 In Your Own Voice	1½–2½ hours

4 Lecture
    Before the Lecture
    Lecture
    After the Lecture
	
	1–1½ hours
	1–1½ hours
	½–1 hour

WHAT CAN BE SKIPPED?

Each chapter of *Academic Listening Encounters* is structured to maximize students' understanding of the chapter topic. As mentioned, vocabulary and ideas recycle through the four sections, as students move through a chapter. However, it is certainly possible to skip sections that do not address your students' needs. You may want to emphasize listening, in which case you can eliminate many or all discussion tasks, as well as Section 3 (In Your Own Voice). If you want to emphasize discussion over speeches, you can skip the oral presentations in Section 3 while still doing the other activities in that section. Depending upon the focus of your course, you can use only the lectures, or only the interviews. The first listening activity is a content preparation for the chapter, but can be skipped to save time. You can also save time by completing vocabulary exercises, summaries, outlines, etc., as a class rather than having students do them on their own first and then checking answers together.

Chapters or even units can be skipped as well, or done in a different order. Remember that the first time a task appears, it is accompanied by a task commentary box. If you skip chapters or do them out of order, use the task index at the back of the Student's Book to locate the commentary boxes for new tasks.

ADDITIONAL ACTIVITIES

Additional activities are given at the end of each unit in the Chapter-by-Chapter Teaching Suggestions in this Teacher's Manual. Read these suggestions before you start the unit. You may find that you want to insert one of them into the middle of a chapter, depending on your student's response to the material.

TEACHING SUGGESTIONS

SUGGESTIONS FOR RECURRING CHAPTER FEATURES

Section Introductions

Each chapter in the Student's Book is divided into four sections. Each section begins with a brief preview: *In this section you will* . . . Always read these previews together with the class, and answer any questions that arise. Take enough time with this task for all students to contribute.

Tasks and Commentary Boxes

Virtually every activity throughout *Academic Listening Encounters* is presented as a task. Each task practices a specific language or thinking skill critical for high intermediate academic-bound students of English. Most tasks are recycled throughout the book. (See the task index at the back of the Student's Book.) The first time a task title appears, it is followed by a shaded task commentary box containing information about the task. Always read this commentary and check for understanding. Ask students: *What are we doing in this exercise? Why is this useful?*

Listening Tasks

You will notice a headset symbol 🎧 next to certain tasks. This denotes a listening task. Before students listen to the audiotape and complete the task, make sure that students read over the task (for example, the outline, incomplete summary, or list of comprehension questions) and think about what information they will need to listen for.

Replay tape excerpts as many times as you think will benefit the majority of students and enable them to complete tasks successfully, including interviews and lectures.

Use of the Audiotape

A cassette symbol indicates the point at which you should play the audio-tape. Play the tape as many times as you think will benefit the majority of your students. They are not expected to catch every word; it is not necessary.

As an alternative to the tape, you may try reading the lectures to your students. (See the section titled Listening Script in this Teacher's Manual.) Try to incorporate appropriate stress, intonation, and body language. Except for Chapters 4 and 9 (which contain interviews in Section 1), the tape segment for the listening task in Section 1 (Getting Started) can also be read.

Oral Presentations

Section 3 (In Your Own Voice) contains suggestions for oral presentations. While students are presenting, have classmates take brief notes. To keep them on task, you may do the following: Announce that there will be a content quiz on the presentations later. Use your own notes to write one general question about each presentation. Dictate the questions, and allow students to use their notes to answer.

Photos, Cartoons, and Drawings

Some of the art in the Student's Book functions as part of a specific task, but most of it is included to build interest and aid comprehension. Draw students' attention to the art and discuss its connection to the topic. (Specific ideas for discussion are given in the Chapter-by-Chapter Teaching Suggestions in this manual.) The photos and drawings found at the beginning of each unit and chapter are a good vehicle for introducing or reviewing related vocabulary. Explain the vocabulary in the cartoons, and try to elicit explanations.

SUGGESTIONS FOR TEACHING VOCABULARY AND COMPREHENSION

Vocabulary

Unfamiliar vocabulary is a great stumbling block to comprehension, so a great effort has been made to gloss or preteach most of the language that is unfamiliar to intermediate students. In each part of Section 2 (American Voices), have students read the vocabulary and glosses in the box by themselves first; then read the vocabulary items aloud so that students can hear how the words are pronounced. Check for understanding of glosses given in the vocabulary boxes.

Each part of the lecture in Section 4 (Academic Listening and Note Taking) begins with a task called *Guessing vocabulary from context*. First, read the vocabulary aloud. As you do so, encourage students to use context or other clues to narrow down the meaning of each word or phrase. When checking the vocabulary task, always see if a student can pick the correct answer; give the correct answers yourself only as a last resort. Discourage the use of dictionaries: Remind students that as university students their reading load will be so large that there will not be time to look up every unfamiliar word.

Any photos or realia that you can bring to class will help with comprehension and retention of vocabulary.

Comprehension and Discussion Questions

One of the goals of *Academic Listening Encounters* is to develop oral fluency, and for this reason there is a great deal of pair and small group work. If students have communicated successfully in pairs or small groups, they will feel more confident about sharing with the class.

Let students control the all-class comprehension checks or discussions whenever possible. They can divide up the questions, assign each one to a different student or pair of students working together. Use the board, and ask for a student volunteer to do the writing. For opinion questions (e.g., in Section 1, Getting Started, *Reading and thinking about the topic*, Step 3) stress that there are no right or wrong answers. Encourage students to give their own ideas, and model acceptance of all opinions. For comprehension questions – as with vocabulary – give the answers yourself only as a last resort.

Give students plenty of time for discussion questions; circulate and encourage all students to voice their opinions. Whenever possible, pair and group students from different cultures. Move on to the next activity before discussion begins to die out or digress from the subject at hand.

GENERAL TEACHING SUGGESTIONS

Teacher's Role

As much as you can, try to take part as an equal in everything: discussions, paired activities, predicting. Because so many of the tasks in this book are based on students' own knowledge and opinions, you should spend most of your time in the role of a participant or facilitator rather than authority figure. The students should be teaching you as much as you are teaching them.

Suggested Correction Techniques

Academic Listening Encounters uses content to teach listening, note taking, and discussion skills. It is not intended to promote formal accuracy. In correction, stress content over form. If a student makes a form (i.e., grammar or pronunciation) error in oral production that does not interfere with communication, do not correct it. If you do correct a form error, do so indirectly. For example:

Student: *I think friends need to be kindness.*
Teacher: *OK, friends need to be kind, they need to show kindness. Good. What else?*

If the content is incorrect, let peers correct it. If a student writes an ungrammatical response on the board, deal with its content first: *Is it correct?* Then you can have peers suggest grammatical corrections. However, stress that content is the main focus in this course.

Homework

Some of the activities in *Academic Listening Encounters* can be done at home. For example, students can read and then think or write about given discussion questions, and they can do the *Guessing vocabulary from context* exercise before the lecture. They can also do the After the Lecture comprehension tasks at home, using the notes they took while listening to the lecture. Interviews and surveys are normally done outside of class time.

Testing

The lecture in each chapter may be used as a listening test. Play the tape (or read the lecture) once or twice, as best suits the level of your students and have them take notes while they listen. Quizzes on the content of the lectures can be found in the Lecture Quizzes section of this manual. These quizzes can be photocopied and passed out for students to complete using their notes.

CHAPTER-BY-CHAPTER TEACHING SUGGESTIONS AND ANSWER KEY

UNIT 1
Mind, Body, and Health

UNIT TITLE PAGE

Go over the three terms in the unit title to be sure that students understand them. Elicit related terms, like *mental* and *physical*.

Read the unit summary paragraph with students and make sure that they understand all the language. Have them look ahead in Chapter 1 and locate the sections mentioned in the paragraph: the interviews with a teacher (Nancy) and a police officer (Sam), and the lecture on the link between mind and body (*Stress and the Immune System*). Elicit the meanings of *stress* and *immune system*. Ask, *Which term relates to the mind? Which relates to the body?*

CHAPTER 1
The Influence of Mind Over Body

1 GETTING STARTED (pages 2–3)

Read the first paragraph with students. Talk about what a *relaxation exercise* is.

Reading and thinking about the topic

Ask students to think about why the statement in the commentary box is true. (We read some of the same words and think about some of the same ideas that we will hear, so we can anticipate them.)

1➤–3➤ After Step 1, elicit or give explanations of terms that students may not know, such as *inescapable*, *hassles*, and *cope with*. Proceed with Steps 2 and 3.

Answers (page 2)

2➤ *1* major: loved one's death, divorce

minor: waiting in line, getting stuck in traffic jams

2 Stress affects the immune system.

3 learn to handle and relieve stress

3

Examining visual material

Elicit from students ways in which pictures, charts, facial expressions, etc., help us to understand a message. (If needed, demonstrate facial expressions showing such emotions as confusion, fear, and fatigue, and have students identify what you are expressing.) Then have students complete the task in the text.

🎧 Listening to directions

Elicit examples of when we have to follow oral directions (for example, in a routine physical examination). Point out that this task is a listening task, as indicated by the headsets.

1➤–3➤ Do Steps 1 and 2 with students. Give them about two minutes to write their responses in Step 2. Then circulate among different groups as students do Step 3. Share what you wrote and listen to what they wrote. With the whole class, elicit responses to questions 1 and 2.

---

2   AMERICAN VOICES: Nancy and Sam *(pages 4–7)*

Have students look ahead at the pictures of Nancy and Sam. Ask if students know any elementary school teachers or police officers.

BEFORE THE INTERVIEWS

Predicting the content

Elicit a definition of *predicting*. Have students do Step 1 alone. After Step 2, write students' responses on the board to summarize their ideas.

INTERVIEW WITH NANCY: The stress of teaching
first-graders

Read the vocabulary items in the box aloud so that students will hear how they are pronounced. Answer any questions.

🎧 Personalizing the topic

1➤–3➤ After students read the pamphlet excerpt in Step 1, discuss terms that may be unfamiliar, such as *boredom* and *things go wrong*. Before you play the tape, point out that it is not necessary to understand every word of the interview. Students should listen for the symptoms mentioned in the pamphlet excerpt.

Answers *(page 5)*

1➤ The following items should be checked in the boxes as "Frequent Signs of Too Much Stress."

_____ Increased boredom and great fatigue ☑

_____ Increased feelings of anger when small things go wrong ☑

_____ Frequent colds and infections ☑

🎧 Listening for specific information

Elicit examples of specific information that students listen for in their daily lives (for example, homework assignments, test dates, and weather forecasts).

1➤–3➤ Have students read the comprehension questions in Step 1 and try to answer them based on what they remember from the first listening. Then go over their answers as a class. Accept all answers as possible, but do not confirm any at this point. This will help to focus students' listening. Then proceed with Steps 2 and 3.

Answers (page 5)

1➤ **1** for 20 years; 3-year-olds, preschool, and elementary school

2 Children bring problems to class; one disruptive child can disturb the entire class; a teacher cannot forget about work when she goes home.

3 She has to be very patient all day with her class.

4 She works very closely with the children, and they often have colds or flu; teaching is stressful, and stress can lower one's resistance to illness.

5 She exercises regularly and talks to her friends.

INTERVIEW WITH SAM: The stress of being a police officer

Review what students said was stressful about being a police officer in *Predicting the content*, on page 4 of the Student's Book. Read the vocabulary items in the box aloud so that students will hear how they are pronounced. Answer any questions about definitions.

🎧 Listening for specific information

1➤–3➤ After students read the comprehension questions in Step 1, review the meaning of *cope with* and *deal with* in questions 4 and 5. Proceed with Steps 2 and 3. Play the interview again if you feel most students would benefit from it.

Answers (page 6)

1➤ **1** for 25 years

2 Patrol is the most stressful assignment because of the fear factor. A patrol officer never knows how people will react to being stopped.

3 Police officers have more everyday illnesses, ulcers, and heart disease than the average adult.

4 exercise programs, psychological counseling, and discussion groups

5 He's a baseball fan, he gets daily exercise, and he has a good relationship with his wife.

AFTER THE INTERVIEWS

Comparing information from different sources

Elicit some examples of different sources of information – for example, newspaper articles, books, pamphlets, and the Internet.

1▶–2▶ After students read the pamphlet excerpt, discuss terms that may be unfamiliar, like *support system* and *send negative signals*. Then proceed with Step 2. Point out that *both* Nancy and Sam follow some of the suggestions.

Answers (page 7)

1▶ Nancy: Become part of a support system; take care of your health.
Sam or the LAPD: Become part of a support system; take care of your health; make time for yourself. It may also be inferred that the LAPD teaches patrol officers to anticipate stressful situations (the routine traffic stop).

Drawing inferences

Explain *inference*. As an example, act the part of a person on the phone, saying, "Oh, hello, Bob. . . . No, not yet, but I have three job interviews today." The inference that can be made from listening to one side of the conversation is that the person you hear is probably looking for a job.

1▶–2▶ Students may not agree on all statements, and they do not need to. If there is disagreement on any statements, have the whole class give reasons on both sides of the argument.

Answers (page 7)

1▶ The following are the most likely answers.

_D_ **1**	_A_ **5**
_A_ **2**	_D_ **6**
_A_ **3**	_A_ **7**
_A_ **4**	

---

3   IN YOUR OWN VOICE *(page 8)*

Ask for an explanation of *research*.

Collecting data

Ask for a synonym of *data* (information).

1▶–2▶ Before students do Step 1, refer them to the photograph of the emergency room workers on page 8 in the Student's Book to get them started. Circulate and help with vocabulary. Then in Step 2, consolidate lists on butcher paper or on the board. Before voting, give students time to defend their choices.

Giving an oral presentation

Stress the importance of speaking from brief notes, rather than reading or memorizing a prepared speech, written out word-for-word. (A memorized speech usually sounds belabored, and the language is often too difficult for listeners to follow. A read speech simply does not communicate well.) Give students a brief model speech in which you report on an interview with a colleague on the stress of being an English teacher.

1➤–*2*➤   Have students work in pairs. They can do Step 1 outside of class if this is preferable. Encourage them to ask for specific details and to take good notes on what their partner says. Try to make Step 2 as stress free for students as possible. Tell them to limit their speech to 3 or 4 minutes. After each presentation, ask questions on points you did not understand. Encourage the student audience to do the same. After all students have spoken, ask for generalizations – for example, ask, *What were the most frequently mentioned symptoms of stress?* As students are speaking you can make brief notes on individual students' content, pronunciation, grammar, use of eye contact, appropriateness of language, and so on. Write up your notes and give them to students later as feedback on their presentations.

4 ACADEMIC LISTENING AND NOTE TAKING:
Stress and the immune system *(pages 9–14)*

Discuss what a lecture is and how it is different from an interview. Elicit a definition of *psychology* (*psych-* "mind" + *-logy* "study"). Review the meaning of *immune system*. Discuss what kind of research a psychology professor would probably be presenting. Ask, *Who does this kind of research?*

BEFORE THE LECTURE

Building background knowledge on the topic

1➤–*4*➤   Read Step 1 along with students. Ask how many subtopics the lecture will contain (four). Students do not need to understand what these subtopics mean yet. Before they read Step 2, ask if anyone has ever heard of Ivan Pavlov and can give any information about his experiments with dogs. Read Step 2 along with students. Have volunteers try to reconstruct what Pavlov did, without trying to use the terms *conditioned/unconditioned* and *stimulus/response*. Then proceed with Steps 3 and 4.

Answers *(page 9)*

3➤   Food (*an _unconditioned_ stimulus*) naturally makes a dog salivate (*an _unconditioned_ response*). If we always ring a bell (*a _conditioned_ stimulus*) as we feed the dog, after a while the dog will salivate even without the food (*a _conditioned_ response*).

🎧 *Note taking: Using telegraphic language*

With students listening and following along, read the commentary box. Stop and check for comprehension as you read.

1▶–4▶ Tell students that they are going to do a listening exercise to practice using telegraphic language. What they will hear is taken directly from the lecture, so it will give them a preview of the lecture content. Proceed with the task. In Step 4, elicit the correct matches from Step 2 first; then have students volunteer to write their telegraphic notes on the board. Have the class orally reconstruct the original ideas from the notes, without referring to the sentences in Step 1.

Answers (pages 10–11)

1▶–3▶ Abbreviations will vary.

2	*a*	Rsrch. shows: stress hurts imm. syst.
4	*b*	Drs. etc. now say: mind may cure better than drugs
1	*c*	Many health probs. come from mind (psychosomatic)
3	*d*	Rsrch. shows: sick + feel helpless → worse health

LECTURE, Part One: Psychoneuroimmunology and animal studies on stress

Help students break down the word *psycho-neuro-immuno-logy*. See if they can identify any of its parts, but do not try to explain the term. It will be defined in the lecture. Ask students to guess what is meant by *animal studies on stress*. Ask, *What kind of animals might these studies involve? What kind of stress?*

Guessing vocabulary from context

Stress the importance of developing the ability to guess from context: The reading load at a university is so great that there is simply not time for students to look up all unfamiliar words. Furthermore, meaning is so dependent on context that a dictionary sometimes confuses matters.

1▶–2▶ Do the first item as an example. Elicit the correct answer; then see if students can explain how they chose the answer. Proceed with Steps 1 and 2. Students do not need to check their answers in their dictionaries unless they are in doubt.

Answers (page 11)

1▶ 1   *a*
     2   *b*
     3   *b*
     4   *b*
     5   *c*
     6   *a*
     7   *c*

🎧 *Summarizing what you have heard*

Underscore the importance of being able to write a summary. Ask for examples of different professionals who are required to write summaries (secretaries, health care workers, engineers, reporters).

1➤–4➤ For Step 1, answer any vocabulary questions. Elicit guesses as to what might go in the blanks, but do not confirm or reject any of them. Proceed with Steps 2 and 3. In Step 2, encourage students to listen for and take notes on the important points, which are the ones included in the summary. Replay the tape if you think doing so will be beneficial for most students. After Step 4, go over the summary as a class. Answer any questions about differences in wording.

Sample answers (page 12)

1➤ Wording will vary. Alternatives are given in brackets.

STRESS AND THE IMMUNE SYSTEM, Part One

There is a lot of evidence to support the idea that our minds can affect our _bodies_ . Many of the health problems that people suffer, such as headaches, _high blood pressure_ , and _ulcers [heart disease, skin rashes, high cholesterol]_ , may be related to psychosomatic disorders – that is, they may be caused by the _mind_ .

The new field of *psychoneuroimmunology* (PNI) studies the way in which our minds can affect our _immune systems_ . In a healthy person, the immune system protects the body against _disease_ . Animal and human research has shown that stress – especially uncontrollable stress – can hurt the immune system.

Robert Ader did an important study with rats in which he learned, quite by accident, that the rats' _immune systems_ could be conditioned to _malfunction_ . This was an exciting discovery for science: if the immune system can be taught to _malfunction_ , that probably means that it can also learn to _get better [heal itself]_ .

LECTURE, Part Two: Human research in PNI

Ask what *PNI* stands for. Ask students to guess what is meant by *human research*. Given Part One of the lecture, on what will the human research in Part Two be focusing?

Guessing vocabulary from context

1➤–2➤ See the teacher's notes for *Guessing vocabulary from context* under LECTURE, Part One.

Answers (page 13)

1➤ 1 _c_   4 _c_
 2 _a_   5 _a_
 3 _a_

🎧 Summarizing what you have heard

Point out to students that in this task they will practice the same skill as in Part One of the lecture.

1▶–4▶ See the teacher's notes for *Summarizing what you have heard* under LECTURE, Part One.

Sample answers (page 13)

1▶ Wording will vary. Alternatives are given in brackets [ ].

STRESS AND THE IMMUNE SYSTEM, Part Two

There are also *human* studies to support the idea that the mind can *influence the body [affect the immune system]*. Just *thinking* about stressful situations can suppress the *immune system*. This has been seen in studies on accountants before tax time, and on *students* before *exams*. Also, if people feel out of control, this can compromise their *immune systems*. Studies show that people in nursing homes who didn't choose to *be there* are more likely to get sick than people who *did*.

People in the *health care [medical]* field are becoming more interested in PNI. We see this, for example, in the treatment of headaches and *sleeplessness [high blood pressure]*. More doctors and nurses today are teaching their *patients* to control these problems by using *relaxation techniques* rather than medication.

AFTER THE LECTURE

Sharing your cultural perspective

Point out that the research cited in the lecture and also the people interviewed in this chapter are Western. Other cultures may have a very different perspective on the connection between mind and body. Have students in pairs or small groups discuss questions 1 and 2. If time permits, ask for volunteers to share part of their discussion with the class.

Comparing information from different sources

Remind students that they have already done a task of this type on page 7 in the Student's Book. After students have read the cited findings, check for understanding. Then proceed with a discussion of questions 1 and 2. Encourage students to contribute opinions based on their experience.

CHAPTER 1 Lecture Quiz

See the Lecture Quiz section at the back of this manual for a photocopiable quiz on the lecture for Chapter 1. Quiz answers can be found on pages 145–149.

CHAPTER 2

Preventing Illness

Turn back to the Unit 1 title page (page 1 in the Student's Book) and reread what it says about Chapter 2. Point out that *staying healthy* is a paraphrase of *preventing illness*. Have students look ahead in Chapter 2 and locate the interviews with two former smokers (Pat and Donna), and the lecture on keeping the heart healthy (*Risk Factors in Cardiovascular Disease*).

---

1   GETTING STARTED (pages 15–16)

Talk about what *experiment* and *heart rate* mean.

Reading and thinking about the topic

1➤–3➤   After Step 1, elicit or give explanations of terms that students may not know, such as *genetics*, *boom*, *aerobic*, and *cardiovascular*. Proceed with Steps 2 and 3.

Answers (page 15)

2➤ **1** *Possible answer*: Health is the most important thing that you can have.
  2 Fewer people are smoking, and more people are exercising.
  3 medical evidence and research

Recalling what you already know

Remind students that this textbook is all about human behavior, and as humans, they already know a great deal about the topic! Tell them that throughout the book, they will be asked to draw on their own background knowledge. Then proceed with the task.

Answers (page 16)

  1 how fast the heart beats
  2 Put your finger on your wrist or neck and count the beats.
  3 Blood is pushed through the heart.
  4 It gets faster when we are using our muscles and when we feel excited or afraid.

Listening to directions

Point out to students that this is the experiment mentioned at the start of the chapter.

1▶–3▶   Do Steps 1 and 3 with students. Circulate as students do Step 2.

Answers (page 16)

2▶   **1** Yes, because the heart was pumping extra blood to the muscles. Blood carries oxygen, and the muscles needed extra oxygen to do the extra work.
  2 *Possible answers*: When we are in a stressful situation, when we are afraid, or when we are doing something fun and exciting, the heart rate increases.
  3 In general, a slow heart rate indicates a healthier heart.

---

2   AMERICAN VOICES: Pat and Donna *(pages 17–22)*

Have students find the pictures of Pat and Donna (pages 18, 19, and 20). Ask if they know anyone who has stopped smoking or who is trying to quit.

BEFORE THE INTERVIEWS

Predicting the content

1▶–2▶   Have students share their answers to the questions in Step 1: you or the students can write them on the board or on butcher paper. Alternatively, assign one question each to four different pairs of students, who then gather answers from classmates and summarize the results.

INTERVIEW WITH PAT: How he started smoking, and how he finally quit

Read the vocabulary in the box aloud. Answer any questions. For *peer pressure*, check for understanding of the cartoon. Ask students what kind of peer pressure is being illustrated in the cartoon.

🎧 *Restating what you have heard*

Elicit some examples of paraphrases; (e.g., *I think it would be good for you to give up cigarettes. = You should stop smoking.*) Emphasize the importance of being able to paraphrase. Point out that it's possible to simply repeat a string of words without having any idea what it means. To show that you really understand what you have heard or read, you need to be able to restate the idea in different words.

1▶–3▶   After students read the incomplete summary, elicit what kind of information will probably go in the blanks – for example, numbers. Proceed with Steps 2 and 3. Replay the interview if you feel most students would benefit from it. Then answer any questions about acceptable wording or paraphrases in the summary.

1➤   Wording will vary. Alternatives are given in brackets.

Pat was <u>13</u> or <u>14</u> years old when he started smoking. He smoked about <u>20 to 30</u> cigarettes a day. Pat smoked cigarettes, and later a <u>pipe</u>, for a total of <u>25</u> years. He tried to <u>stop [quit]</u> many times. In high school, he gave up cigarettes while he was on the <u>basketball</u> team, but he <u>started smoking</u> again after the <u>last [final]</u> game. Pat finally quit smoking in <u>1983</u> because he had a <u>heart attack</u>. He has <u>never</u> been tempted to <u>start smoking</u> again.

INTERVIEW WITH DONNA, Part One: How she started smoking, and how she tried to quit

Read the vocabulary items in the box aloud for pronunciation. Answer any questions.

🎧 *Restating what you have heard*

1➤–3➤   See the teacher's notes for *Restating what you have heard* under INTERVIEW WITH PAT. Ask for examples of *public places* (in the second paragraph in the box at the top of page 19 in the Student's Book).

1➤   Wording will vary. Alternatives are given in brackets.

Donna started smoking at about age <u>16</u> or <u>17</u>. She and her friends would get together after <u>school</u>. They would eat <u>candy</u> and smoke cigarettes. After a while, Donna was smoking a <u>pack</u> a day. She kept smoking for <u>13</u> more years.

Donna studied in South <u>America</u>, and later she taught in <u>Mexico</u>. In both places, smoking was <u>more</u> common than in the United States. People smoked in public places, for example, in <u>movie theatres</u> and <u>classes [supermarkets, taxicabs, buses]</u>. When Donna returned to the United States, she went to <u>graduate</u> school. She and her friends would drink <u>espresso [coffee]</u> and smoke <u>Gauloises [French cigarettes]</u>.

But Donna wasn't feeling very <u>well [healthy]</u>. She had chronic bronchitis. She tried to quit many times but could not. Later, when she was married and <u>pregnant</u>, she nearly stopped. But as soon as her <u>son</u> was born, she <u>started smoking again</u>.

INTERVIEW WITH DONNA, Part Two: How she stopped smoking, and how her life has changed

Read the vocabulary items in the box aloud for pronunciation. Answer any questions.

🎧 Restating what you have heard

1➤–3➤   See the teacher's notes for *Restating what you have heard* under INTERVIEW WITH PAT. Elicit an explanation of *hypnotherapist*.

Sample answers (page 20)

1➤   Wording will vary. Alternatives are given in brackets.

> Finally, a friend of Donna's recommended a hypnotherapist. This friend had been a very heavy smoker – 3 packs a _day_ – but the hypnotherapist had helped him _quit_. Donna decided to go and get hypnotized herself, and the treatment _worked_ [_was successful_]!
>
> Donna believes that she was able to _quit_ this time because _she had reached the point where she was ready_. Donna's _son_ was _very happy_ when she quit because he had always _worried_ about her _health_. Soon, Donna started to feel _better_ physically. She noticed that she had a lot more _energy_, and she could _smell_ things again. Also, food started to _taste better_ to her. A final advantage was _money_ [_financial_].
>
> After she quit, Donna decided to _save_ all of the _money_ that she had been spending on _cigarettes_ and buy _healthy_ gifts for herself and her son. Exactly one _year_ after she quit smoking, she bought them _mountain bikes_ [_bicycles_]. She has continued _to use the money for something healthy every year_ [_buy healthy gifts every year_].

AFTER THE INTERVIEWS

Hearing versus inferring

Review what an *inference* is from page 7 in the Student's Book.

1➤–2➤   Do the first question of the chart in Step 1 with students as an example. After Step 2, ask students if they have any answers that are different from their partners'. Ask them to explain their reasoning.

Answers (page 21)

1➤   The answers designated as inferences (**I**) may vary.

	Pat	**Donna**
Why did you start smoking?	a, b, c (I)	a, b, c (I)
How long did you smoke?	c	a
What physical problems did smoking cause?	a, b (I), c (I), d (I)	b, c, d
What method(s) did you use to try to quit?	a	a, b, c
Do you ever feel like smoking now?	b	b (I)

Examining graphic material

Before students do the task, ask them to give examples of everyday information presented in graphic form (e.g., postal rates, bus schedules, opinion polls, population growth rates). Then proceed with the questions. Have students share answers as a class.

Answers (page 22)

1 France
2 India
3 In all cases, more men than women smoke.
4–5 *Answers will vary.*

---

3   IN YOUR OWN VOICE *(pages 23–24)*

Ask for examples of other habits besides smoking that can affect health either negatively or positively.

Sharing your cultural perspective

If time permits, have the class share opinions and reasons for the final segment of question 3. Students could also prepare and present an informal debate on this question.

Conducting a survey

Ask for an explanation of the difference between a survey and an interview (a survey is designed to get answers to only a few questions from many people; interviews usually ask more questions of an individual person). Conduct a one-question survey in your class to illustrate. For example, introduce the topic of breakfast. Ask students to think of a possible question. (For example: *How often do you eat breakfast?* Answers: *Always/Usually/Sometimes/Almost never/Never*.) Poll the class and record answers on the board as shown in Step 3 in the Student's Book, including gender and, if applicable, nationality.

Then have the class analyze the data. First, have them express the results in percentages. Next, have them answer these questions: *How often do most students eat breakfast? Is there a difference depending on gender and, if applicable, nationality?*

behavior, survey. Students can also conduct opinion surveys, or a combination of the two.

1▸–2▸ Allow students to pursue a topic of their choice, but make sure that the choice is not too broad. For ESL students, comparisons between their eating, exercise, and sleep habits at home and abroad can be very interesting. Or they may want to test a hypothesis about the relationship between two factors, such as sleep habits and health, or exercise and stress. They may also want to compare students to nonstudents, or native speakers of English to nonnative speakers.

Have students write some survey questions about their topic for homework. Then use a class period for students to fine-tune their survey questions by asking them to one another and to you. Check for grammar and language use.

3▸–4▸ Give students 3 to 5 days to conduct their surveys outside of class and to analyze their data. If you have colleagues in your school who are willing, arrange for students to visit different classes and to do their surveys during class time. When students have finished their analyses, tell them that they will not have time to present the results of every question in their report to the class; they should report on their most interesting or unexpected findings. Encourage them to try to explain what they think the results mean. Also, ask them to suggest other questions they would ask if they were to repeat the survey. If possible, provide paper for students to create graphs to illustrate their findings. You could also ask students to turn in a written summary or an outline of the results.

---

4 ACADEMIC LISTENING AND NOTE TAKING:
Risk factors in cardiovascular disease *(pages 25–30)*

Ask for an explanation of *risk* and *factors*. *Cardiovascular* will be defined in the following task.

BEFORE THE LECTURE

Building background knowledge on the topic: Vocabulary

Talk about the advantages and challenges of using an English-English dictionary.

1▸–2▸ Have students do Step 1 alone.

Answers (page 25)

2▸ *1* referring to the blood vessels
2 An artery carries blood *from* the heart whereas a vein carries blood *to* the heart.

Predicting the content

Review the meaning of *predicting*.

1➤–2➤ Help students with vocabulary related to illnesses. A diagram of the human body would be helpful.

🎧 *Note taking: Using symbols and abbreviations*

With students listening and following along, read the commentary box. Stop and check for comprehension as you read. Ask students for examples of other symbols or abbreviations that they know (*UN, USA, CIA*, etc.).

1➤–4➤ For Step 3, have students use their own paper to take notes. You or a student volunteer could take notes on the board for one of the excerpts in Step 3. Review notes as a class after Step 4. Have students compare symbols and abbreviations.

Answers (page 27)

1➤

m	*1*
l	*2*
j	*3*
k	*4*
e	*5*
d	*6*
o	*7*
f	*8*
a	*9*
c	*10*
i	*11*
h	*12*
n	*13*
b	*14*
g	*15*

Sample answers (page 27)

3➤ Wording and abbreviations will vary.

1 *CVD = ♥ attack, stroke, PVD*
2 *♂ ↗ risk for CVD (♀ ↘ risk)*
3 *Obese = ≥ 20% over ideal wt.*
4 *Early ♥ attack prob. "Type A" pers. (get angry, work, & play hard) = ↗ risk of CVD.*

LECTURE, Part One: Unalterable risk factors in CVD

Ask what *unalterable* means and what *CVD* stands for.

Guessing vocabulary from context

1▸–2▸ Read the directions for Step 1 and give an illustration of how much we can figure out about an unfamiliar word from studying its context. For example, *Consider the word* deleterious *in this sentence: Smoking has a deleterious effect on health. What kind of word is* deleterious? (adjective) *Does it mean something good or something bad?* (probably something bad) Encourage students not to look at the definitions in Step 2 until they have told their partners as much as they can about the words in Step 1. Check matches as a class after Step 2.

Answers (page 28)

1▸

k	1
j	2
h	3
g	4
a	5
b	6
e	7
i	8
c	9
d	10
f	11

Outlining practice

With students listening and following along, read the commentary box. To check their comprehension, ask students what an outline looks like. Have them explain how it is different from notes.

1▸–4▸ After students read the incomplete outline in Step 1, check for understanding of symbols and vocabulary. Proceed with Steps 2 through 4. Circulate and check outlines.

Sample answers (page 29)

1▸ Wording will vary.

RISK FACTORS IN CARDIOVASCULAR DISEASE, Part One

I. CVD = heart attacks, strokes, peripheral vascular disease
    A. ♥ attack = *part. or complete block'g of artery to ♥ muscle*
    B. *Stroke* = *block'g of 1 or more arteries to brain*
    C. PVD = *peripheral vascular disease – "clots to legs"*
II. Unalterable risk factors
    A. Gender: Before age 50, ♀ *are protected by estrogen:* ↘ *risk for CVD than* ♂
    B. Age: older = ↗ *risk for CVD*
    C. *Diabetes* = ↗ *risk for CVD – reason not known.*
    D. *Family history: usually too high cholesterol – can be hereditary.*

LECTURE, Part Two: Alterable risk factors in CVD

Ask what *alterable* means, and have students guess what some alterable risk factors for CVD might be.

Guessing vocabulary from context

1➤–2➤ See the teacher's notes for *Guessing vocabulary from context* under LECTURE, Part One.

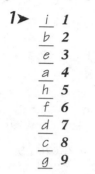

Answers (page 29)

1➤

_i_	**1**
_b_	**2**
_e_	**3**
_a_	**4**
_h_	**5**
_f_	**6**
_d_	**7**
_c_	**8**
_g_	**9**

🎧 Outlining practice

1➤–4➤ See the teacher's notes for *Outlining practice* under LECTURE, Part One.

Sample answers (page 30)

1➤ Wording will vary.

RISK FACTORS IN CARDIOVASCULAR DISEASE, Part Two

III. <u>Alterable risk factors</u>
  A. HBP – Controlled w/ <u>medicat'n – few side effects</u>
  B. <u>Obesity</u> (≥20% <u>over ideal weight</u>) may → <u>diabetes</u> and <u>HBP</u>
  C. <u>Cigarette smok'g</u> ↗<u>CVD</u>
  D. <u>Stress</u>
    Type A pers. (= <u>perfectionist, easily angry, competitive, work/play hard</u>)
    Hostility → ↗ <u>risk of ♥ disease.</u>
  E. Sedentary lifestyle (= <u>no exercise</u>) → ↗<u>risk of CVD</u>

AFTER THE LECTURE

Sharing your personal and cultural perspective

Remind students that the distinction between "Type A" and "Type B" personalities is a Western idea, and thus it may not be valid in their cultures. Encourage them to contribute opinions based on their own perspectives and experiences.

CHAPTER 2 Lecture Quiz

See the Lecture Quiz section at the back of this manual for a photocopiable quiz on the lecture for Chapter 2. Quiz answers can be found on pages 145–149.

Additional Ideas for Unit 1

1 Watch the movie *The Doctor*, starring William Hurt as a brilliant surgeon who has no interest in his patients' hearts, minds, or feelings until he becomes seriously ill himself. Have students discuss how it relates to this unit.

2 Have a health care professional come in and talk in detail about one or two of the risk factors mentioned in the lecture in Chapter 2 and answer students' questions about them.

3 Find current newspaper or magazine articles related to smoking. Assign different articles to small groups. Have them read and summarize the articles for the class.

4 Invite a police officer, firefighter, or another professional with a stressful job to your class to talk about work stress. (Whenever I have a police officer come and talk to my students, they usually want to ask questions along the lines of *Do you really give more speeding tickets to red cars*? I suggest having each student prepare two questions: one about stress and the other about whatever else they really want to know. Do the stress questions first.)

5 Have students go to the library or search online for more information about the link between stress and illness. Someone may want to find out more about Ader's research on the immune system, or about studies linking depression and illness. A student could also look for a fuller explanation of Pavlov's experiments with dogs. Have students give brief reports to the class on what they have learned.

UNIT 2
Development Through Life

UNIT TITLE PAGE

Read the unit title and ask students what kind of development takes place through life (physical, mental, social).

Read the unit summary paragraph with students and make sure that they understand all the language. Have them look ahead in Chapter 3 and locate the sections mentioned in the paragraph: the interview with an adolescent girl (Jora) and her father (Eric), as well as the lecture on the kinds of problems that adolescents sometimes have (*Common Problems of Adolescents in Mental Health Treatment*). Ask what *mental health* means and what *treatment* is.

CHAPTER 3
Adolescence

1 GETTING STARTED (pages 32–33)

Ask what *growth rate* means.

Reading and thinking about the topic

1➤–3➤ After Step 1, elicit or give explanations of terms that students may not know, such as *challenging parental control*, *attitudes*, and *disobey*. Proceed with Steps 2 and 3.

Answers (page 32)

2➤ **1** physical and emotional changes
2 *Possible answers*: pushing for more independence, challenging parents' control, experimenting with different attitudes or opinions, disobeying parental rules
3 No. Teenagers need support, guidance, and rules.

21

Examining visual material

Have partners summarize, in one statement, what they notice about James's and Sarah's changes in height.

🎧 Recording numbers

Elicit from students examples of different kinds of numbers they have to record quickly in everyday situations (addresses, telephone numbers, dates, prices). For the *Recording numbers* task, students will need a pen and pencil, or two pens of different colors, so make sure that students are prepared before they start to listen.

1▸–3▸ Before Step 1, check to see that students understand the measuring system and symbols used in the graph (' = feet, " = inches). Proceed with the rest of the task. Pause the tape if necessary for students to fill in information on the graph.

Answers (page 33)

1▸ The following information should be recorded on the graph:

James	Sarah
at age 10 – 4'10"	at age 10 – 4'9"
at age 14 – 5'1"	at age 12 – 5'4"
at age 16 – 5'8"	at age 15 – 5'8"
at age 18 – 5'11"	at age 18 – 5'9"
at age 21 – 6'	
at age 22 – 6'1"	

---

2 AMERICAN VOICES: Jora and Eric (pages 34–38)

Check for understanding of the expression *let someone do something*. Ask students for examples of what their parents didn't let them do when they were 13 or 14 (go on dates, wear earrings, stay up late on weeknights, etc.).

BEFORE THE INTERVIEW

Sharing your cultural perspective

1▸–2▸ Circulate and check for understanding as students do the task. Then allow students to share their answers with the class if they like.

INTERVIEW WITH JORA AND ERIC, Part One: Freedom and responsibility

Read the vocabulary items in the box aloud for pronunciation. Answer any questions.

🎧 *Listening for specific information: Script writing*

1➤–3➤ After students complete Step 1, explain that the incomplete scripts in their books present two past conversations that Jora and Eric *recall* in this interview. Students will not hear these conversations verbatim on the tape.

Sample answers (page 35)

1➤ Wording will vary. Alternatives are given in brackets.

Jora: Dad, can you drive *us to a concert at 10:30* tonight?
Eric: I can drive you there, but I can't pick you up. How will you *get home*?
Jora: We can *take a cab* [*taxi*].
Eric: *No, that's too dangerous.*

. . .

Jora: Dad, why are you so strict!? You never give me any *freedom*!
Eric: Jora, I'll give you more *freedom* when you show me that you can *handle it*.
Jora: How can I do that?
Eric: Well, for example, if I ask you to *do something*, you need to *do it* [*get it done*]. Or if you are in any kind of trouble, *you need to call me*.

INTERVIEW WITH JORA AND ERIC, Part Two: Clothes and makeup

Read the vocabulary in the box aloud and answer questions. Check for understanding of *gangs*. Draw a picture or show a photograph of *bell bottoms*.

🎧 *Listening for main ideas*

The commentary box introduces the idea that in conversation people express themselves gradually, in bits. This means that their main points are sometimes not stated directly.

1➤–3➤ After students read the statements in Step 1, check for understanding of the vocabulary. Proceed with Steps 2 and 3.

Answers (page 36)

1➤ 1 *doesn't agree*
2 *stricter*
3 *and so is Eric*
4 *sometimes*
5 *but Eric does*

INTERVIEW WITH JORA AND ERIC, Part Three: Different parents, different rules

Read the vocabulary in the box aloud. Ask students for examples of *chores* they had to do as adolescents. Ask if they received an *allowance*.

🎧 *Summarizing what you have heard*

1▶–3▶   After Step 1, ask students to share their predictions. Do not reject or confirm any. Proceed with Steps 2 and 3. As students are completing the summary in Step 2, remind them that they do not need to use the same words they heard in the interview.

Sample answers (page 37)

1▶   Wording will vary. Alternatives are given in brackets.

Jora agrees that her father is _strict_, but _fair_. When he won't let her do something, at first she is _angry_, but later she usually _understands [sees his point of view]_. Jora's mother (who is divorced from Eric) is _less_ strict than Eric about some things, such as _movies_. Jora says that Eric won't let _her watch PG-13_ movies, but her mother _rents R-rated movies and lets her watch them_. However, her mother is stricter about _chores_, _junk food_, and _money [buying things for Jora]_. For example, she wants Jora to pay for _her friends' presents_. In conclusion, Jora says that Eric lets her do " _just enough_."

AFTER THE INTERVIEW

Drawing inferences

1▶–2▶   Students may have different opinions on some of the statements, and they do not need to agree on the answers. Encourage students to justify their inferences.

Sample answers (page 38)

1▶   Answers may vary.

_A_ **1**
_D_ **2**
_D_ **3**
_A_ **4**
_A_ **5**

Looking at the cultural context

Ask what is meant by *the broader picture*, as this phrase is used in the commentary box. Ask students if they think Jora is a typical teenager or not. Would she be considered typical in their culture? If not, why not?

1▶–2▶   Students could also answer the questions in Steps 1 and 2 in writing.

3 IN YOUR OWN VOICE *(page 39)*

Review the meaning of *research*. Ask for different ways that research can be done (interviews, surveys, reading, listening to taped material, watching videos).

Sharing your personal perspective

Circulate and help students with their questions. Actual interviewing may be done outside of class, or allow 10 to 15 minutes of class time for the interview. You may want students to write a short follow-up report, or have the class pool their answers, survey-style, to one or two general questions, such as *Were your parents too strict, just right, or not strict enough?*

Giving an oral presentation

Go over the pointers on giving speeches. You may also want to review the guidelines for oral presentations given in the commentary box on page 8 in the Student's Book.

1➤–3➤ Help students think of someone they could interview. In an EFL setting, they may need to interview someone in their native language, and then translate what they learned into English. Give feedback on questions.

4 ACADEMIC LISTENING AND NOTE TAKING: Common problems of adolescents in mental health treatment *(pages 40–45)*

Elicit from students what a *psychotherapist* is.

BEFORE THE LECTURE

Predicting the content

1➤–2➤ As students are doing the task, circulate and help with vocabulary.

Looking for causes

1➤–2➤ After students read Step 1, check for understanding of vocabulary. In Step 2, use the board to list possible causes.

🎧 Note taking: Using space to show organizational structure

With students listening and following along, read the commentary box. Stop and check for comprehension as you read. Ask a student to show on the board what *indenting* is.

1➤–4➤ After Step 1, make sure that students understand the abbreviations in the notes. Then proceed with Steps 2 through 4. Remind students to save their notes.

Sample answers (page 41)

3➤ Indented notes with suggested spacing:

2nd prob – school (= failing, acting out, not going to class)
   reasons
      younger bros. & sisters – parents busy
      teens have diffic. – need to rely on parents
   treatment
      get parents more involved
      par. need to give <u>structure</u>
         clear rules for behav.
         discipl. if teen breaks rules

LECTURE, Part One: Adolescent alcohol and drug abuse

Guessing vocabulary from context

1➤–2➤ Encourage students not to look at the definitions in Step 2 until they have told their partners as much as they can about the words in Step 1. Check matches as a class after Step 2.

Answers (page 42)

1➤

g	1
m	2
f	3
e	4
a	5
j	6
b	7
n	8
c	9
k	10
d	11
l	12
i	13
h	14

Note-taking practice

1➤–4➤ After Step 1, ask about the structure of Part One of the lecture, as shown in the student notes. Ask the following questions: *How many problems will the lecture discuss?* (two) *How many will be presented in the first part of the lecture?* (one) *How many general points will be presented about the problem, and what are they?* (two: *reasons* and *treatment*). Then proceed with Steps 2, 3 and 4. Check as a class.

Sample answers (page 43)

1➤ Wording will vary.

Common probs. of adols. in mental health treatment (Pt. 1)

Discuss 2 problems of adols.
    = <u>drug/alcohol abuse</u> & <u>probs. at school</u>
Talk abt. reasons, then possible <u>treatm't</u>
1st prob. = <u>Addict'n to alcohol/drugs</u>
    Reasons = usually <u>physically/sexually abused</u>
        Adol. takes drugs to <u>escape from negative feelings ab't themselves or abuse</u>
    Treatment = <u>long</u> & difficult
        Hospital 1st: <u>need to detoxify</u>
        Group work: <u>help adol. get coping skills to resist drugs</u>
        After 30 – 60 days, adol. ready to <u>talk</u>. May feel <u>guilty or angry</u>
            Important! Therapist must <u>not judge – permit adol. to feel any feel'gs</u>
            Takes a long time: <u>feelings are blunted by drugs/alcohol</u>
            If teen can <u>stay sober in treatm't</u>, good chance <u>for recovery</u>

LECTURE, Part Two: Common problems related to school

Have students take out the notes they copied in Step 3 of the task *Note-taking: Using space to show organizational structure* on page 42 in the Student's Book. Tell students that the notes are for Part Two of the lecture. Ask students, *According to the notes, what common problems related to school can you expect to hear about in Part Two of the lecture?* (failing, acting out, and not going to class)

Guessing vocabulary from context

1➤–2➤ See the teacher's notes for *Guessing vocabulary from context* under LECTURE, Part One.

Answers (page 44)

1➤

<u>b</u> 1		<u>e</u> 5
<u>f</u> 2		<u>g</u> 6
<u>h</u> 3		<u>a</u> 7
<u>d</u> 4		<u>c</u> 8

🎧 Note-taking practice

1➤–3➤ After students have read over their notes from *Note-taking: Using space to show organizational structure*, ask about the structure of Part Two of the lecture. Ask the following questions: *How many problems will be presented?* (one) *How many general points will be presented about the problem, and what are they?* (two: *reasons* and *treatment*). Tell students that they will hear a more complete version of Part Two this time. Tell them to listen for extra details, and for a conclusion. Then proceed with Steps 2 and 3. Go over their notes as a class, especially the conclusion.

Sample answers (page 44)

2➤ Wording will vary.

> Common probs. of adols. in mental health treatment (Pt. 2)

2nd prob. – school = (failing, acting out, not going to class)
    Reasons
        Younger bros. & sisters – parents too busy with younger sibl'gs – not giving
           adol. enough attn.
        Other poss. reason = parents are too involved – need to let teens prove themselves
    Treatm't
        Get parents involved = parents need to give _structure:_
           1. clear rules for behav.
           2. discipl. if teen breaks rules
               e.g., let teen fail if doesn't do HW
        Therapist's job = help parents find correct level of involvem't in adol.'s life
    Conclusions : Adolesc. probs. come mostly from home lives – no surprise
        Teens struggle with identity: Who am I? What can I do?
        Need family to give nurtur'g/source of identity

AFTER THE LECTURE

Sharing your cultural perspective

Share results of the discussion as a class if time permits.

Considering related information

1➤–2➤ See if students know what *Newsweek* magazine is. Bring an issue to class if possible. After Step 1, explain any unfamiliar terms, such as *poll* and *worship*.

CHAPTER 3 Lecture Quiz

See the Lecture Quiz section at the back of this manual for a photocopiable quiz on the lecture for Chapter 3. Quiz answers can be found on pages 145–149.

Adulthood

Turn back to the Unit 2 title page (page 31 in the Student's Book) and reread what it says about Chapter 4. Ask for a definition of *adulthood* and its more common related noun/adjective (*adult*). Have students look ahead in Chapter 4 to In Your Own Voice, where they will see pictures of people of different ages. Point out that in this chapter there is a survey rather than interviews. Review the difference. Then have students locate the lecture, *Developmental Tasks of Early Adulthood*.

1 GETTING STARTED (pages 46–47)

Review the meaning of *stages*.

Reading and thinking about the topic

1➤–3➤ After Step 1, elicit or give explanations of terms that students may not understand, such as *transition, spouses*, and *rewards*. Proceed with Steps 2 and 3.

Answers (page 46)

2➤ **1** young adulthood, middle adulthood, and late adulthood
  2 Young adulthood is the time for many important decisions. In middle adulthood, we face physical changes and changes in our family. In late adulthood, we continue to change physically. Our children have left home, and people in our age group begin to get sick and die, but we have more free time.

Predicting the content

1➤–2➤ Encourage students to imagine themselves at these different ages or to think of people they know who are middle-aged, elderly, etc. Do not take time to share predictions as a class here.

🎧 Recording numbers

1➤–4➤ Before Step 1, read through the names and identify gender. (Bruce, David, Otis, and Gene are male.) Proceed with the task. Put students in charge of organizing the survey process in Step 4.

▸ *Answers (page 47)*

1▸

Name	Age Now	The Best Age
Bruce	28	late 20s
Julie	25	4–9
Ann	57	30s
David	45	his age now
Otis	70	25–30 years ago
Laurie	68	her age now, 40s
Gene	71	he doesn't know
Loleta	77	from college graduation to marriage

---

2   AMERICAN VOICES: The best age to be *(pages 48–51)*

BEFORE THE SURVEY

Predicting the content

Circulate and listen to students' reasons as they do the task. Then allow students to share their reasons with the class if they like.

SURVEY, Part One: Bruce, Julie, and Ann

Have students refer to their answers on page 47 of the Student's Book to find out the ages of the people being surveyed in this part. Give an example of how we use *actually* as it is defined in the vocabulary box.

🎧 *Answering true/false questions*

Give examples of true negative statements (e.g., *I'm not speaking Farsi now*) and of false statements that are partially true (e.g., *Sunday is just after Friday and just before Monday*).

1▸–3▸   After students complete Step 1, answer any questions about the meaning of the statements. Then proceed with Steps 2 and 3.

▸ *Answers (pages 48–49)*

1▸
1	T
2	F
3	T
4	F
5	T
6	T
7	T
8	T
9	F

SURVEY, Part Two: Otis, Laurie, and Gene

Have students refer to page 47 of the Student's Book to find out the ages of the people being surveyed in this part. Read the vocabulary in the box and answer questions.

🎧 *Summarizing what you have heard*

1▶–3▶   After Step 1, ask students to share predictions about what goes into the blanks. Proceed with Steps 2 and 3. While students are doing Step 3, circulate and help with grammar.

Sample answers (page 50)

1▶   Wording will vary. Alternatives are given in brackets.

Otis is a retired university professor. He says that his best teaching years were between _35_ and _50_ because he was more open to new ideas, he _lectured better_, and _he read a lot more_. At the age of _50_, he created _four new courses_. However, Otis feels that in another sense, his last _10_ years have been the best because _he has become more mature [more responsible and sensitive to the world around him]_.

Laurie and Gene are married. They are both painters. Laurie remembers her _40s_ as a great time because she got her master's degree, she _had more time to paint_, and _she started studying music_.

Gene says that the older he gets, the _more he thinks about his youth_. Especially when he wakes up in the morning, he notices that _he doesn't feel so well [his bones and his joints hurt]_. He and Laurie talk about how long _it takes them to get going in the morning_. When he was a young man, in the Army, he used to _get up and be ready in 10 minutes_. But now _it takes a long time_.

AFTER THE SURVEY

Creating a chart

Ask students why a chart is a good way to record information (easy to see at a glance), and what information is best presented on a chart (short answers, such as numbers). This task may be done with a master chart on the board or on a large piece of paper. Assign each age category to a small group of students. Have each group discuss what its members heard or inferred from the survey and have groups record their answers on the master chart.

Sample answers (page 51)

Childhood	no worries, no responsibilities
Teens	most difficult time, worst time
20s	start to have responsibilities, have a plan, can be a stressful time, new decisions
30s	feel settled, know what you like
40s	time for your own interests, professionally very productive, free of responsibilities
50s	do more for yourself
Late adulthood	physical problems, more mature and responsible, more aware of the world

3   IN YOUR OWN VOICE (page 52)

Ask students how their *cultural perspective* could make a difference in how they view adulthood.

Sharing your cultural perspective

Circulate and help students formulate their ideas. Point out that some characteristics of adulthood may be common to all cultures. Students should record similarities as well as differences. You may want to have students write their generalizations on the board.

Conducting a survey

1▸–2▸ Review with students how to record survey answers. Refer them to page 24 in the Student's Book. Ask if it is considered impolite to ask a person's age in their culture. Discuss how they can determine and record a person's age (guess; write *early 40s*; etc.). Give students a day or two to collect their data, add up the answers, and convert them into percentages (*40 percent of the people surveyed . . .*). As an extra activity, compile the raw data as a class and come up with overall percentages. Put the students in charge of the process.

4   ACADEMIC LISTENING AND NOTE TAKING:
Developmental tasks of early adulthood *(pages 53–58)*

Review what a *psychotherapist* is. Discuss what ages *early adulthood* refers to and, as a class, think of what important decisions and life changes (*developmental tasks*) a young adult has to make.

BEFORE THE LECTURE

Building background knowledge on the topic

1➤–3➤   Do Steps 1 and 2 with the class. Answer vocabulary questions as they arise. Proceed with Step 3, and check answers as a class.

Answers (page 53)

3➤   *1*   *Possible answers*: by moving away from home, by getting a job
2   He was a psychologist who studied the development of the human personality throughout life.
3   It means *in opposition to* or *against*. *Intimacy* and *isolation* are opposites.
4   *Intimacy* is the forming of close relationships with others. *Isolation* is the inability to relate closely to others, a feeling that we cannot depend on anyone else.

Note taking: Paying attention to signal words

With students listening and following along, read the commentary box. Stop and check for comprehension as you read. Ask students for other examples of *signal words*.

1➤–4➤   Explain that the words in items 1–7 in Step 1 are quotations from the lecture. Then have students proceed with the task. Circulate and offer guidance as students complete Step 4.

Answers (pages 54–55)

1, 3➤   Notes will vary.

b	**1**	*life changes pers. must make to grow & dev.*
c	**2**	*finan'ly, emot'ly, & socially*
b	**3**	*solely as parents*
e	**4**	*often diffic. to live w/o finan. help fr. parents*
d	**5**	*diffic. for young adult to establ. finan. indep. fr. parents.*
a	**6**	*separ. is crisis time for family*
f	**7**	*two import. tasks of yng. adult.*

LECTURE, Part One: Separation from parents

Guessing vocabulary from context

1➤–2➤ Encourage students not to look at the definitions in Step 2 until they have told their partners as much as they can about the words in Step 1. Check matches as a class after Step 2.

Answers (page 55)

1➤

b	**1**
f	**2**
a	**3**
e	**4**
d	**5**
c	**6**
g	**7**

🎧 *Note-taking practice*

1➤–3➤ After Step 1, check for understanding of the abbreviations used in the notes. Ask how many tasks will be discussed (one), and how many points will be made about the task(s) (four). Then proceed with Steps 2 and 3.

Sample answers (page 56)

1➤ Wording will vary.

Developmental tasks of young adulthood (Pt. 1)

Young adulthood = from early or *mid-20s*
    in Western culture, young adult should be financially, *emot'ly* , & *soc'ly* indep.
    from *parents* .
1st task = separate from *prnts.* & create new rel'ship based on *mutual adulth'd.*
    – process really began *in early childh'd*
    – happening later in US today because of *job competit'n – diffic. to be finan. independ.*
    – not always successful: *some chldrn. keep role of child, & prnts. keep par. role*
    – crisis time because *big change in fam. – frighten'g*

LECTURE, Part Two: The crisis of intimacy versus isolation

Review what is meant by *intimacy versus isolation* (see the answers in *Building background knowledge on the topic* under BEFORE THE LECTURE).

Guessing vocabulary from context

1➤–2➤ See the teacher's notes for *Guessing vocabulary from context* under LECTURE, Part One.

◢ *Answers (page 56)*

1▶
_d_	**1**
_e_	**2**
_h_	**3**
_b_	**4**
_g_	**5**
_f_	**6**
_c_	**7**
_a_	**8**

🎧 *Note-taking practice*

1▶–3▶ After Step 1, check for understanding of the abbreviations used in the notes. Then proceed with Steps 2 and 3. After Step 3, discuss the cartoon. Ask how it relates to the lecture topic.

◢ *Sample answers (page 57)*

1▶ Wording will vary. Alternatives are given in brackets.

Developmental tasks of young adulthood (Pt. 2)

2nd task – traditionally leads to _marriage._
    *called "crisis of _intimacy vs. isolation_"
    If child develops _healthy_ identity in adolescence → able to
     join with [_make a commitment to_] another pers. in young _adulth'd._
        – person must be able to compromise, _sacrifice_ , _negotiate_ .
        – if successful → _intimacy (closeness, connection)_
        – if not succ. → _isolation (alone, self-absorbed)_
        – success depends on _develop. of healthy ident. in late adolesc._
    Alternative to marriage today: staying single longer
        have freedom _to take risks, move to different area_
        skepticism _about marriage_
        → wait until _late 20s or older_ → much lower _divorce rate_
If young adults succeed at these 2 tasks → _future success & satisfaction_ [happiness]

AFTER THE LECTURE

Applying general concepts to specific data

Check for understanding of *abstract concept* and *specific data*. What abstract concepts were presented in the lecture? (separation from parents and intimacy versus isolation)

1▶–2▶ Check answers as a class after Step 1. Proceed with Step 2. Circulate and encourage guessing.

Answers (page 58)

1► Bruce and Julie are young adults.

Answers (page 58)

2► **1** People are getting married later.
        2 The fact that more Americans are living alone and the rise in the divorce rate could be interpreted as evidence that Americans today have more trouble establishing intimacy.

Sharing your personal and cultural perspective

1►–2► Share opinions as a class if time permits.

CHAPTER 4 Lecture Quiz

See the Lecture Quiz section at the back of this manual for a photocopiable quiz on the lecture for Chapter 4. Quiz answers can be found on pages 145–149.

Additional Ideas for Unit 2

1 There are a number of movies that deal with adolescence or adulthood. Here are some examples of movies for students to view and discuss in light of the topics covered in this unit:

- *The Breakfast Club*, starring Ally Sheedy and Molly Ringwald, is about a group of teenagers who get in trouble in school.
- *Heathers* is about the cruel world of high school cliques.
- *Two Friends* is about two very different high school girls whose friendship falls apart.
- *Big*, starring Tom Hanks, is about a 13-year-old boy who gets his wish to be "big." The movie gives us a very funny look at the trials of both adulthood and adolescence.
- *On Golden Pond*, with Henry Fonda, Katharine Hepburn, and Jane Fonda, deals with the process of growing old.

2 As a class, visit a junior high school or high school class and either observe or interview the students. If your class is going to do interviews, help them prepare some general "get-acquainted" questions beforehand. If they are observing, have them discuss beforehand what they want to look for. (For example: *Are the girls wearing makeup? Is everyone wearing a similar style of clothing? Are there obvious cliques?*)

3 Arrange a visit to a nursing home. Have students in pairs interview people about their lives. Help them write questions beforehand. Some possible questions: *What period of your life has been the best? the most exciting? Do you have any regrets? What advice would you give to a young person? What do you like about your present age?*

UNIT 3
Intelligence

UNIT TITLE PAGE

Read the unit title and ask students for words related to *intelligence*.

Read the unit summary paragraph with students and make sure that they understand all of the language. Have them look ahead in Chapter 5 and locate the sections mentioned in the paragraph: the interview with the author's childhood friend (Ruth), as well as the lecture on the history of intelligence testing (*Intelligence Testing – An Introduction*).

CHAPTER 5
Assessing Intelligence

1   GETTING STARTED *(pages 60–61)*

Discuss what a *standardized test* is.

Reading and thinking about the topic

1➤–3➤   After Step 1, elicit or give explanations of terms that students may not know, such as *vary*, *capacity*, and *resourcefulness*. Proceed with Steps 2 and 3.

Answers *(page 60)*

2➤   *1* the capacity to understand the world and the resourcefulness to deal with its challenges

 2 People are not sure what they really measure and how they should be used.

🎧 Listening to directions

1➤–4➤   Before students listen to the tape, tell them that this "test" will not be graded. It's just for fun. Do Step 1 along with the class. Replay the tape after Step 2 if you think students would benefit. After Step 3, share guesses as a class. Do Step 4 along with the class.

Answers (page 61)

1➤ Some answers may vary.

1 Cairo
2 Call 911(Emergency); get the neighbors out of their house if they are home.
3 225 km
4 girl – 3; boy – 7
5 2-4-8-3-9-1-6-5
6 6-2-3-4-8-7
7 Both are forms of transportation, travel on the ground, need fuel, carry people, touch the ground at four points, and are expensive to buy and keep.
8 3   1   4   2
9 Prejudice is an attitude or feeling – usually negative – that a person has about something, someone, or a group of people before he or she has enough information to make a fair judgment.

Sample answers (page 61)

3➤ 1 general information
2 world knowledge, common sense
3–4 mathematics
5–6 memory span
7 ability to find similarities
8 time order, understanding the whole from its parts
9 vocabulary

---

2   AMERICAN VOICES: Ruth *(pages 62–66)*

Given the chapter topic, have students guess at what kinds of school memories Ruth and the author will be discussing.

BEFORE THE INTERVIEW

Personalizing the topic

1➤–2➤ Circulate and check for understanding as students do the task. After Step 2, allow students to share their answers with the class if they like.

INTERVIEW WITH RUTH, Part One: Being a "smart kid"

Read the vocabulary items in the box aloud and discuss *irregular* spellings – they are very common in English! Ask students if spelling is ever irregular in their languages. Discuss the cartoon on page 63 in the Student's Book and explain what a *spelling bee* is (a game in which people are asked to spell words aloud and are eliminated when they misspell a word). Demonstrate *I threw my hands up*.

🎧 Listening for specific information

1➤–3➤ Students may write short answers on their own paper. After Step 3, check as a class.

Answers (page 63)

1➤ **1** the first reading group
    2 how to spell words
    3 He is two years older.
    4 irregular spellings
    5 She made up little songs to remember the spellings.
    6 no

INTERVIEW WITH RUTH, Part Two: A subject she "didn't get"

Review the meaning of *I don't get it*. Have students try to predict what subject Ruth "didn't get." Ask for the literal meaning of *label*; elicit how this usage derives from it.

🎧 Listening for specific information

1➤–3➤ See the teacher's notes for *Listening for specific information* under INTERVIEW WITH RUTH, Part One.

Answers (pages 63–64)

1➤ **1** In seventh grade (junior high school), she started to have trouble with algebra.
    2 She just "floundered through" and decided that she was not good at algebra.
    3 She had close friendships with several mathematics majors.
    4 She labeled herself as someone who could not do math. She did this in junior high.

INTERVIEW WITH RUTH, Part Three: An incorrect label

Elicit a definition of *sarcasm* when students encounter it in the vocabulary box in the definition of *It must be true!* Give or ask for examples of the use of sarcasm.

🎧 Retelling

Ask students if they have ever had someone repeat back to them what they have said (frequently done when getting directions, phone numbers, credit card numbers, addresses, etc., over the telephone).

1➤–3➤ After Step 3, have volunteers retell the story for the class.

Sample answers (page 64)

1➤ Information that should be included in the reconstruction of Part Three:

1 He took a test that incorrectly labeled him as having very low intelligence.

2 He took a low-paying job. Later, he took another test that showed that he was very bright. His whole life changed.

3 He always had the same intelligence but, because of the suggestive power of a "test," he never doubted the results of the first test – the one that labeled him as unintelligent.

AFTER THE INTERVIEW

Summarizing what you have heard

1➤–*2*➤ Students need not use the same words. Circulate and help with grammar and spelling. After Step 2, go over possible answers as a class.

Sample answers (page 65)

1➤ Wording will vary. Alternatives are given in brackets.

Ruth did very *well* in all her school subjects until she encountered *algebra* in *seventh grade*. She didn't *understand it [get it]*, and she didn't know how to *ask for help [work at it]* because this was the first time that she *had encountered something she didn't understand*. Surprisingly, in college Ruth had many *friends who were math majors*, and she really enjoyed *talking with them [their way of thinking]*, but even though she was good at *talking about math*, she was not good at *doing it on paper*. Ruth believes that she *labeled* herself in junior high school as a person who *couldn't do math [wasn't good at math]*.

   Ruth read about a *man* who had done the same thing, based on the results of *a test* in high school. The man was labeled a *dunce*. He believed the label, and after high school he *got a low-paying job*. Years later, he took another test that showed *him to be very intelligent*. When the man heard this, he *completely changed his life and became a successful businessman*.

Considering related information: Correlation

Point out to students that correlation is a complex measure, and that they do not need to understand it in depth. There may well be students in the class who do; if so, enlist their help in answering questions! It may be worthwhile to give a simplified example: If we imagine a group of students studying English, and we say that they all learn five new vocabulary words every day, we can then say that there is a perfect correlation (1.0) between the size of their vocabulary and the length of study. If this obviously unrealistic correlation existed, then we could predict with complete accuracy how many words the students would know at the end of a week, a month, a semester, etc. Correlations are almost never perfect, but the closer a correlation is to 1.0, the stronger it is. The larger the study, the lower the value required for a correlation to be considered significant – that is, not just the result of chance. For example, in a study involving 100 testees, a correlation as low as .25 is significant.

1➤–2➤ Students choose to be either A or B in Step 1. B students should turn their books upside down and look only at their own table. Before students begin, go over the correct way to say decimal values out loud. For example, .35 is read as "point three five." Also point out that all the correlation values in this table are significant. After Step 2, have each pair of students write one or two statements on the board.

Sample answers *(page 66)*

2➤ • IQ test results are a good indicator of mental retardation.
  • Most people in high-status occupations also have high IQ test scores.
  • If you know a person's IQ test score, you can predict with equal accuracy his/her parents' education level, his/her own school grades, and the level of his/her job.
  • IQ scores are not a very strong predictor of career success.
  • A person's IQ score is a good indicator of how many years of schooling he/she has had.

---

3   IN YOUR OWN VOICE *(page 67)*

Elicit a definition of *limits*, and ask students to think about what the limits of intelligence testing might be.

Sharing your personal and cultural perspective

1➤–3➤ Circulate and answer questions as students are doing Step 1 in pairs. (These questions could also work well as writing prompts.) Read through the questions in Step 2 as a class and check for understanding.

Gathering data

1➤–2➤ Help students think of someone they could interview. In an EFL setting, they may need to interview a teacher in their native language and then translate into English what they have learned.

---

4   ACADEMIC LISTENING AND NOTE TAKING:
Intelligence testing – an introduction *(pages 68–71)*

Ask students what kind of information they expect to hear when they see the words *an introduction*. Ask what *current development* means.

BEFORE THE LECTURE

Predicting the content: Writing information questions

Name a famous historical event, such as a war, and ask students for examples of information questions about it.

1➤–3➤ As students do the task, circulate and help with vocabulary. If they are having trouble working alone, allow them to do Steps 1 and 2 with a partner, and then Step 3 with another pair of students.

Sample answers (page 68)

2➤ • Who first developed intelligence tests?
• Why were intelligence tests first developed?
• What are intelligence tests supposed to measure?
• Where was intelligence testing first used?
• How has intelligence testing changed over the years?
• What problems are there with intelligence testing today?

🎧 Note taking: Recognizing examples

With the students listening and following along, read the commentary box. Stop and check for comprehension as you read. Give a general statement and elicit examples from the class (*Young adults face many decisions; for instance, . . .*).

1➤–3➤ After Step 1, ask volunteers to reconstruct the five points aloud from the abbreviated notes. Then proceed with Steps 2 and 3.

Sample answers (page 69)

1➤ These are some sample notes containing examples.

1	*good mem., reason'g skill, verbal comp. skill*
2	*memory task – 5-yr-old should remember 3 wds., 7-yr-old 5 wds., etc.*
3	*# of tsks. ave. 5-, 6-, 7-yr-old, etc., can do*
4	*child 9 1/2 – w/ mental age 7: IQ = 7 ÷ 9.5 = .74 × 100 = 74 (IQ)*
5	*they have diff. kind of intell: "street smarts" – books & IQ not import. in that environ.*

LECTURE, Part One: A history of intelligence testing

Guessing vocabulary from context

1➤–2➤ Encourage students not to look at the definitions until they have tried to guess the general meaning of the words. Check matches as a class after Step 2.

Answers (page 69)

1▶
_g_	**1**
_h_	**2**
_i_	**3**
_d_	**4**
_b_	**5**
_c_	**6**
_a_	**7**
_f_	**8**
_e_	**9**

🎧 Outlining practice

1▶–4▶ After Step 1, ask about the structure of Part One of the lecture, as shown in the outline. Ask the following questions: *How many main points will be presented?* (one: history) *How many general points will be presented under* history, *and what are they?* (two: Alfred Binet and Lewis Terman). *What do they mean?* (They are proper names.) Then proceed with Steps 2 through 4. Check outlines as a class.

Sample answers (page 70)

1▶ Wording will vary.

INTELLIGENCE TESTING – AN INTRODUCTION, Part One

I. History
    A. Alfred Binet – _began modern intell. testing – France 1905_
        1. Purpose of test = _identify child'n who needed special help – bel'w aver._
        2. Theory behind test = _intell. increases w/ age – older = smarter_
        3. "Mental age" = _age when the aver. child could do a certain # of tasks_
    B. Lewis Terman – _Stanford prof. 1911 – revised Binet's test to use w/ older people_
        Stanford-Binet test – _gives a ratio measure of intell. – still used today_
          a. IQ formula = _divide mental age by chron. age (yrs. & mos.) times 100 = IQ._
          b. Purpose of test = _identify child'n who will have prob. in school_

LECTURE, Part Two: Current approaches and some problems

Ask students what they think *current approaches* means. Ask, *What kinds of problems might the lecturer discuss?*

Guessing vocabulary from context

1▶–2▶ See the teacher's notes for *Guessing vocabulary from context* under LECTURE, Part One.

> *Answers (page 70)*

1➤ $\dfrac{f}{}$ **1**
    $\dfrac{b}{}$ **2**
    $\dfrac{g}{}$ **3**
    $\dfrac{e}{}$ **4**
    $\dfrac{c}{}$ **5**
    $\dfrac{d}{}$ **6**
    $\dfrac{a}{}$ **7**

🎧 Outlining practice

1➤–4➤   After Step 1, ask about the structure of Part Two of the lecture, as shown in the outline. Ask the following questions: *How many main points will be presented?* (two) *How many points will be presented under the second main point, and what are they?* (two: definition and bias). Then proceed. Check outlines as a class.

Sample answers (page 71)

1➤   Wording will vary. Alternatives are given in brackets.

INTELLIGENCE TESTING – AN INTRODUCTION, Part Two

II. Current approaches to intelligence assessment
    A. Wechsler Scales = *dev. by David Wechsler, 1939 – 3 tests for differ. age grps.*
        Different from Stanford-Binet:
        1. *easier to give [administer]*
        2. *test other abilities, e.g., puzzles, visual-spatial*
III. *Some prob. with IQ testing*
    A. Definition: *what is intell.? What does IQ score predict? not related to life success.*
    B. Bias: *Educ. mid/upper class people ↑ IQ scores – test doesn't measure intell. in differ't (nonschool) environ.*

AFTER THE LECTURE

Sharing your personal and cultural perspective

Share results of the discussion as a class if time permits.

CHAPTER 5 Lecture Quiz

See the Lecture Quiz section at the back of this manual for a photocopiable quiz on the lecture for Chapter 5. Quiz answers can be found on pages 145–149.

CHAPTER 6

Accounting for Variations in Intelligence

Turn back to the Unit 3 title page (page 59 in the Student's Book) and reread what it says about Chapter 6. See if someone can explain what *to account for* means. Ask what *variations in intelligence* means. How would these variations be measured? Have students look ahead in Chapter 6 to American Voices and locate the interview with a public school administrator (Dennis). Check for understanding of *administrator*. Then have students locate the lecture on factors influencing the development of intelligence (*Intelligence – Nature or Nurture?*). Review the meaning of *factors* (as in the Chapter 2 lecture, *Risk Factors in Cardiovascular Disease*).

1 GETTING STARTED (pages 72–73)

Explain that the SAT is a standardized test designed to show how well students will do at the university level. Most colleges and universities in the United States require SAT scores as part of the application process.

Reading and thinking about the topic

1➤–*3*➤ After Step 1, elicit or give explanations of terms that students may not know, such as *controversial*, *mental tasks*, and *measurable differences*. Proceed with Steps 2 and 3.

Answers (pages 72–73)

2➤ 1 *Nature* refers to what we inherit from our parents. *Nurture* is what we get from our environment.
2 Research shows that both nature and nurture influence the formation of intelligence.
3 No, there are no measurable differences on general IQ tests.

⌒ Recording numbers

For this task, students will need a pen and pencil, or two pens of different colors, so make sure that students are prepared before they start to listen.

1➤–*3*➤ After Step 3, allow students to share their reactions to the SAT score results as a class. As an extra speaking activity, have students reconstruct the audio script for a partner, using their own graphs.

Answers (page 73)

2➤ The following numbers should be marked on the charts:

	'72	'76	'80	'84	'86	'88	'92	'96
Verbal Scores – Males	531	513	507	510	515		504	507
Verbal Scores – Females	529	508	499	498	504		496	503
Math Scores – Males	527	520	515	519		522	521	527
Math Scores – Females	489	474	473	478		483	484	492

---

2 AMERICAN VOICES: Dennis *(pages 74–78)*

Ask for an explanation of *performance* in the context given. Ask what age groups Dennis works with (roughly ages 6 to 15, since he works with elementary and junior high school students).

BEFORE THE INTERVIEW

Predicting the content

1➤–2➤ As students do Step 1, circulate and answer any vocabulary questions they may have. If time permits, share answers as a class.

INTERVIEW WITH DENNIS, Part One: Gender differences

Ask students what they think the title of Part One means in the context of this chapter. Read the vocabulary items in the box aloud. Answer any questions.

🎧 Listening for specific information

1➤–3➤ Check answers as a class after Step 3.

Sample answers (page 75)

1➤ Wording will vary. Alternatives are given in brackets.

   1 Dennis has been working in public schools for <u>23</u> years.
   2 He has done most of his teaching at the <u>elementary</u> level.
   3 Girls do better in the first years of school because they acquire <u>language</u> and fine motor skills <u>earlier than</u> boys, and they generally <u>behave better</u>.

4 When they want to get the teacher's attention in class, boys are more likely to *do something unexpected* *[or a little inappropriate]*, while girls generally *do a good job on their homework* or *raise their hands in class*.

5 Girls start to "dumb down" in middle school because *they want to be attractive to [and get attention from] boys*.

INTERVIEW WITH DENNIS, Part Two: Different expectations

Elicit a definition of *expectations*. (Ask students to think about the verb *to expect*.) Elicit guesses as to what Dennis means by "different expectations" by asking, *Whose expectations? Expectations of whom?* Read the vocabulary items in the box aloud. Answer any questions.

🎧 *Listening for specific information*

1➤–3➤ Check answers as a class after Step 3.

Sample answers (page 75)

1➤ Wording will vary.

1 According to cognitive research, when a teacher asks a question very quickly, the student being questioned *usually cannot think of the answer right away*.

2 Research shows that when traditional high school math teachers ask questions, they tend to *give boys slightly more time to answer before calling on another student*.

3 Researchers believe that math teachers do this because *they unconsciously expect the boys to be able to answer, so they are willing to wait longer than they would wait for girls*.

INTERVIEW WITH DENNIS, Part Three: Factors affecting school performance

Have students guess at what factors might affect how a child performs in school. Read the vocabulary items in the box aloud. Answer any questions.

🎧 *Listening for specific information*

1➤–4➤ After Step 3, check answers as a class. As students do Step 4, circulate and answer questions: Some of their answers may be correct even though they were not directly stated in the interview.

Sample answers (page 76)

1➤ Wording will vary. Alternatives are given in brackets.

1 Dennis has observed that in general, if parents have money and think that education is important, their children _do well_ _[do better]_ in school.

2 Dennis taught at a school where the students came from very _different [varied]_ backgrounds.

3 Dennis believes that having a computer at home _gives a child an advantage [helps a child develop thinking skills]_.

4 According to Dennis, not all low-income children do _poorly_ in school, and not all wealthy _children do well_.

5 Dennis cites siblings with similar skills at basketball as evidence to support the idea that _kinesthetic_ intelligence is _inherited_.

AFTER THE INTERVIEW

Applying general concepts to specific data

1➤–4➤ Review the meaning of *general concepts*. Ask the following questions: *What two general concepts are being applied in this task?* (heredity and environment, or nature and nurture) *What specific data are the concepts being applied to?* (the five factors mentioned in Dennis's interview as influences on school performance) This is a fairly abstract task, and students may require some guidance. If students are having trouble, ask them direct questions such as the following: *Is kinesthetic intelligence hereditary (from nature), or do we get it from our environment (nurture)?* Circulate and offer guidance and encouragement as students are doing Step 3.

Answers (page 77)

1➤ _E_ ***1*** *(Answer may vary.)*
_H_ ***2***
_E_ ***3***
_H_ ***4***
_E_ ***5***

Sample answers (page 77)

3➤ *1* When girls reach puberty, they may become more interested in attracting boys than in doing well academically.

2 Dennis sees evidence that kinesthetic intelligence runs in families.

3 Children with computers in their environment have an educational advantage over children without computers.

4 Girls start out doing better than boys in school, partly because they naturally tend to acquire language earlier than boys.

5 A child is likely to do well in school if his or her parents think education is important.

Comparing information from different sources

1➤–2➤ Make sure that students understand the cartoon on page 78 in the Student's Book. Ask them how it relates to the idea of multiple intelligences. After Step 1, check for understanding of the article. Terms such as a *critic of the test*, *plugging in the answers*, and *deliberate* may require explanation. Allow 10–15 minutes for Step 2, and encourage creative thinking.

Answers (page 78)

2➤ *1* Boys have a different test-taking style from girls.
  2 Boys are not as concerned with appropriate behavior and following the rules as girls are. They use "test-taking tricks."
  3 *Answers will vary.*

---

3 IN YOUR OWN VOICE *(page 79)*

Remind students that Dennis talked about *kinesthetic intelligence*. Review what it means. Ask them for examples of famous people who are either kinesthetically intelligent or musically intelligent. Have them do the spatial puzzle at the bottom of the page. (Answer to spatial puzzle: Figure [d]) Tell them to be thinking about their own intelligence and asking themselves what they are naturally good at.

Sharing your personal and cultural perspective

1➤–3➤ After Step 1, you may want to compile answers on the board. Step 2 could be done as a class rather than in small groups. After Step 3, share answers as a class.

Giving an oral presentation

1➤–2➤ This task requires students to broaden their traditional definition of intelligence. Have them think about things their parents or grandparents do well. Ask, *Do you have some of the same talents or interests yourselves?*

---

4 ACADEMIC LISTENING AND NOTE TAKING:
Intelligence – nature or nurture? *(pages 80–84)*

Ask students if they can turn the lecture title into a complete question. Elicit the meaning of *argument* in the context of the opening paragraph. Draw students' attention to the photo of laboratory rats in a maze on page 80 in the Student's Book. Ask, *What are they doing?*

BEFORE THE LECTURE

Predicting the content

1▶–2▶   Before students do Step 1, point out that the indenting in Professor Cash's lecture notes provides a valuable key to the structure of her lecture. Before Step 2, draw students' attention to the photograph of Courtney and Chris Salthouse and the caption below it (page 82 in the Student's Book). Ask if this situation presents evidence for the *nature* argument or the *nurture* argument (or maybe both). After Step 2, go over the questions and let students give their suggestions.

Answers (page 80)

2▶   *1*   Tryon, Hebbe, and Zajonc
　　2   *Sample answer*: The more intelligent rats will be able to solve the problem: They will learn how to get out of the maze or how to get the cheese in the maze (as shown in the picture in the Student's Book); or at least they may be able to find the solution more quickly than less intelligent rats.
　　3   *Sample answer*: With twins, scientists can study people with similar heredity (parents/nature). If twins are raised in different environments, scientists can study how environment affects people with similar heredity. In adoption studies, scientists can study children raised in the same environment but with different heredity (parents/nature).
　　Answers to questions 4–6 will vary.

🎧 Note taking: Recording numbers

With students listening and following along, read the commentary box. Stop and check for comprehension as you read. Ask students if they have ever had trouble understanding and recording numbers, and if so, in what situations.

1▶–3▶   Before Step 1, review the meaning of *correlation* (page 65 in the Student's Book), and how it is expressed (e.g., "point three five"). Proceed with the task. After Step 3, compare answers as a class.

Answers (page 81)

1▶　*a*　.85
　　　b　72
　　　c　6
　　　d　.45
　　　e　15 pts.
　　　f　1.0
　　　g　1940s

LECTURE, Part One: Evidence for the role of nature

Ask students what they expect to hear about in this part of the lecture.

Guessing vocabulary from context

1➤–2➤ Encourage students not to look at the definitions in Step 2 until they have told their partners as much as they can about the words in Step 1. Check matches as a class after Step 2.

Answers (pages 81–82)

1➤
_b_	**1**
_e_	**2**
_g_	**3**
_f_	**4**
_h_	**5**
_a_	**6**
_i_	**7**
_d_	**8**
_c_	**9**

🎧 Listening for specific information

1➤–3➤ This task can be used as a quiz, one in which students can read the questions beforehand so that they will know what to listen for. Or it can be used as an ordinary listening task. If you would like to treat this task as a quiz, you may want to photocopy page 156 at the back of this book and then collect these sheets after students have completed the listening task.

Sample answers (page 82)

1➤ Wording will vary.

INTELLIGENCE – NATURE OR NURTURE? Part One

1 No, there isn't. There is research to support both the nature and the nurture arguments.
2 Tryon's research on rats and maze-learning showed that smart rats produced smart rat babies.
3 Identical twins share exactly the same DNA.
4 Fraternal twins' environments are more similar than those of other siblings because they are exactly the same age.
5 Identical twins raised apart have a lower correlation of IQ scores than those raised together (in the same environment).
6 The IQ scores of adopted children are closer to the scores of their biological parents (nature) than to those of their adoptive parents (nurture).

LECTURE, Part Two: Evidence for the role of nurture

Ask students what they expect to hear about in this part of the lecture.

Guessing vocabulary from context

1▶–2▶ See the teacher's notes for *Guessing vocabulary from context* under LECTURE, Part One.

Answers (page 83)

1▶

e	**1**
d	**2**
a	**3**
b	**4**
c	**5**
f	**6**

🎧 *Listening for specific information*

1▶–3▶ See the notes for *Listening for specific information* under LECTURE, Part One. If you would like to treat this task as a quiz, you may want to photocopy page 156 at the back of this book.

Sample answers (page 83)

1▶ Wording will vary.

INTELLIGENCE – NATURE OR NURTURE? Part Two

1 Hebbe raised one group of rats in a stimulating environment and another group in a boring environment. He then weighed their brains, and he found that the first group had larger, heavier brains. Their environment had made a difference in their brain development.

2 Children will develop higher levels of intelligence (as measured by an IQ test) in an environment where education is valued.

3 Zajonc developed the confluence model to account for the fact that first-born children have higher IQ scores than their younger siblings.

4 The confluence model says that a child's intelligence is formed by the intellectual climate of the home (as measured by the average IQ within the home). The first child grows up in an environment of adult intelligence, but with each successive child, the average IQ is lowered because young children do not contribute very much to the home intellectual climate.

5 decreases in funding for schools, drugs, two working parents, single parenting, day care, food additives, and television

AFTER THE LECTURE

Sharing your personal and cultural perspective

1▶–2▶ This task could also be done in small groups or as an all-class activity. After students read the excerpt in Step 2, check for comprehension and then proceed with the discussion.

Thinking critically about the topic

This is a reminder to students that, indeed, they cannot believe everything they read or hear. As students discuss the questions, circulate and encourage skepticism! Then share ideas as a class.

Sample answers (page 84)

Answers to questions 1 and 3 will vary according to personal opinion and experience.

2 In an extended family household, there would be more adults (uncles, aunts, grandparents, etc.) contributing to the intellectual climate, so the average household IQ would be higher. As a result, the confluence model might predict that children in an extended family would have higher IQs than those in a nuclear family.

CHAPTER 6 Lecture Quiz

See the Lecture Quiz section at the back of this manual for a photocopiable quiz on the lecture for Chapter 6. Quiz answers can be found on pages 145–149.

Additional Ideas for Unit 3

1 There are a number of interesting movies that deal with the topics discussed in Unit 3. Here are two suggestions:

- *Little Man Tate*, starring Jodie Foster and Dianne Wiest, tells the story of a very intelligent young boy and his struggle to have a normal life. Watch the movie and talk about why it is difficult to be different, even in a desirable way.

- *Stand and Deliver* is a powerful and inspiring movie. Based on a true story of Chicano high school students in Los Angeles, it deals with several of the influences on intellectual development that have been discussed in this chapter – for example, the students' socio-economic background and their teachers' expectations. Watch the movie and discuss how it relates to the chapter.

2 Obtain copies of a short aptitude or interest test and allow students to take it (in class or at home) and self-score it. Do not require students to share their scores, particularly on an aptitude test. Such tests are often found in self-help books or popular magazines. Afterwards, discuss what factors might affect test performance.

3 Have students go to the library or search online for more information about one or more of the people discussed in Unit 3, namely, Alfred Binet, David Wechsler, William Tryon, Robert Zajonc, or Howard Gardner. They may also be interested in looking up research on a particular aspect of intelligence, such as the correlation of IQ between twins. Have students give brief reports on what they have learned.

4 Arrange for individual students to observe an elementary school class. As a class, discuss and decide beforehand what they want to look for, for example, differences between the boys' behavior and the girls' behavior or the teacher's style of addressing questions. For comparison, observe a junior high school class as well.

UNIT 4
Nonverbal Messages

UNIT TITLE PAGE

Read the unit title and discuss what *nonverbal* means and what *nonverbal messages* are.

Read the unit summary paragraph with students and make sure that they understand all of the language. Have them look ahead in Chapter 7 and locate the sections mentioned in the paragraph: the interview with three immigrants (Marcos, SunRan, and Airi), and the lecture on nonverbal communication in different cultures (*Body Language Across Cultures*). Discuss the meaning of *body language*.

CHAPTER 7
Body Language

1   GETTING STARTED (pages 86–87)

Ask students to give an example of a *common gesture* used in the United States.

Reading and thinking about the topic

1▶–3▶   After Step 1, elicit explanations of terms that students may not know, such as *convey powerful messages*, *anthropologists*, and *incomprehensible*. Proceed with Steps 2 and 3.

Answers (page 86)

2▶   **1** We use all of our bodies (our faces, our hands, our eyes, etc.).
2 conscious body language: gestures that we use to convey a message, for example, "thumbs up"
3 unconscious body language: things we convey with our bodies without knowing it (*Examples will vary.*)

🎧 Reading nonverbal cues

Give students some examples of nonverbal cues that communicate a clear emotion: surprise, boredom, confusion, etc. Try to move more than one body part. Let students identify the message.

57

1▸–4▸ In a multicultural class, Step 4 may turn into a free-for-all as students teach one another the different meanings of gestures used in their cultures. Enjoy it!

Answers (page 87)

2▸ a <u>4</u>   b <u>6</u>   c <u>5</u>   d <u>3</u>   e <u>2</u>   f <u>8</u>   g <u>1</u>   h <u>7</u>

---

2   AMERICAN VOICES: Marcos, SunRan, and Airi *(pages 88–92)*

If you have students from Brazil, Korea, or Japan, tell them they will be considered "expert informants" and that they may find they do not agree with everything that is said about the body language of their culture. Encourage them to speak up.

BEFORE THE INTERVIEWS

Recalling what you already know

1▸–3▸ Before students do Step 2, encourage guessing. There are no absolute right or wrong answers.

INTERVIEW WITH MARCOS: Brazilian body language

As you read through the vocabulary box with your students, model talking with your hands. In pairs, have students try to talk without using their hands.

⌒ *Answering true/false questions*

1▸–3▸ After Step 3, ask for volunteers to restate the false statements correctly to the class.

Answers (page 89)

1▸ <u>F</u> **1**
    <u>T</u> **2**
    <u>T</u> **3**
    <u>F</u> **4**
    <u>T</u> **5**
    <u>F</u> **6**

INTERVIEW WITH SUNRAN: Korean body language

While reading the vocabulary box with students, show what the *palm*, middle finger, and *index finger* are.

🎧 *Answering true/false questions*

1➤–3➤ See the teacher's notes for *Answering true/false questions* under INTERVIEW WITH MARCOS.

◢ *Answers (pages 89–90)*

1➤
_F_	**1**
_T_	**2**
_F_	**3**
_F_	**4**
_T_	**5**
_F_	**6**

INTERVIEW WITH AIRI: Japanese body language

While reading the vocabulary box with students, demonstrate the hand gesture for "*so-so, sort of.*"

🎧 *Restating what you have heard*

1➤–3➤ Before students listen, have them look at the photograph of Airi at her American sister-in-law's wedding on page 91 in the Student's Book. Ask the following question: *How is Airi's body language different from everyone else's?* After Step 3, go over the paragraph. Answer questions about acceptable wording.

◢ *Sample answers (page 90)*

1➤ Wording will vary.

Airi is married to _an American_, and she has lived in the United States for _nine months_. Airi discovered one difference in body language between Americans and _Japanese_ when she saw herself in a _formal picture_ taken at her _husband's sister's_ wedding. All of the people in the picture were _smiling_ with their _teeth_ showing – except for _Airi_. She felt _embarrassed_ when she saw the picture.

Airi thinks that Japanese and Americans have similar attitudes about eye contact: In both countries, it's good for people to _look at each other_ when they're talking because it shows that they _are really listening_.

Airi has noticed that Americans use more _gestures_ than Japanese. However, Airi says that she is more like an American in this respect: She started using a lot of _gestures_ when she met _her husband_ because it was so difficult to _communicate_.

AFTER THE INTERVIEWS

Thinking critically about the topic

Read over the two important points about body language as a class. Check for understanding. The questions that follow may be answered in small groups if you prefer. Stress to students that they are all experts and everyone's opinion is valid.

Considering related information

1►–2► As students do Step 1, circulate and make sure they are performing the body signals correctly. For Step 2, students choose to be either A or B. B students should turn their books upside down and look only at their own box. After Step 2, ask the class if any of the body signals mentioned have different meanings in their cultures.

3   IN YOUR OWN VOICE *(page 93)*

Ask students how they might go about doing research on body language. Review the different forms that research can take (reading, watching videos, interviewing people, etc.).

Gathering data

1►–4► Have students read through all four steps; then answer any questions that students have. Point out that the term *field research* comes from anthropology, where research is done "in the field" (out in the real world) rather than in a laboratory or a library. Students can do their observations for homework. Make sure that they choose only one aspect of body language to research. Encourage them to include generalizations and cultural comparisons in their report.

Asking for clarification

This task is intended to help students get comfortable with admitting when they do not understand something that is said. Circulate and ask clarification questions of your own. If time permits, have students regroup and repeat the process with students from a different group.

4   ACADEMIC LISTENING AND NOTE TAKING: Body language across cultures *(pages 94–98)*

Ask for an explanation of the lecture title.

BEFORE THE LECTURE

Looking beyond the facts

Point out to students that facts can tend to be dry and boring, and easily forgotten. But if we can relate them to our own experience, they come alive.

1▶–4▶ After Step 2, have students make a master list of nonverbal cues on the board. Demonstrate Step 3 if students are reluctant to proceed.

🎧 Note taking: Mapping

With students listening and following along, read the commentary box. Stop and check for comprehension as you read. Ask if any students have ever used this style of note taking.

1▶–3▶ After Step 3, have students reconstruct the map on the board.

Answers (page 95)

1▶ There are six supporting points and two definitions.

$$\text{"body lang."} \left\{ \begin{array}{l} \underline{posture} \qquad\quad = \ \textbf{how we hold ourselves} \\ \underline{gestures} \qquad\quad = \ \underline{the\ use\ of\ our\ hands} \\ \underline{\textbf{facial expressions}} \\ \underline{eye\ contact} \\ \underline{tone\ of\ voice} \\ \underline{touch} \end{array} \right.$$

LECTURE, Part One: Aspects of body language

Guessing vocabulary from context

1▶–2▶ Students do not need to check their answers in their dictionaries unless they are in doubt.

Answers (pages 95–96)

1▶
<u>c</u> **1**
<u>b</u> **2**
<u>a</u> **3**
<u>c</u> **4**
<u>b</u> **5**
<u>b</u> **6**
<u>a</u> **7**

🎧 *Mapping*

1➤–3➤ Remind students that they have already completed a section of this map in the task *Note taking: Mapping*. Proceed with the task. Check answers as a class.

Sample answers (page 96)

1➤ Some wording will vary.

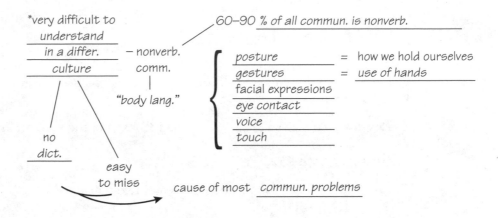

LECTURE, Part Two: Cross-cultural misunderstandings

Ask students what *cross-cultural misunderstandings* are.

Guessing vocabulary from context

1➤–2➤ See the teacher's notes for *Guessing vocabulary from context* under LECTURE, Part One.

Answers (page 97)

1➤
<u>b</u> **1**
<u>c</u> **2**
<u>b</u> **3**
<u>a</u> **4**
<u>b</u> **5**
<u>a</u> **6**

🎧 *Mapping*

1➤–3➤ After Step 1, answer any questions about abbreviations or symbols. Ask the following questions about the structure and content of Part Two of the lecture: *What is the main idea?* (Nonverbal communication causes the most cross-cultural confusion.) *What cultures will be used as examples?* (Japanese culture and American culture.) Then proceed with the task. Check answers as a class.

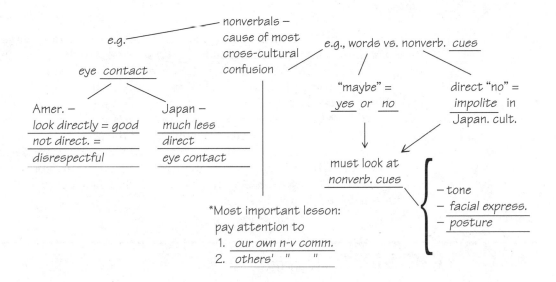

▲ *Sample answers (page 97)*

1➤ Some wording will vary.

AFTER THE LECTURE

Sharing your personal and cultural perspective

1➤–3➤ Share results of the discussion as a class if time permits.

CHAPTER 7 Lecture Quiz

See the Lecture Quiz section at the back of this manual for a photocopiable quiz on the lecture for Chapter 7. Quiz answers can be found on pages 145–149.

The Language of Touch, Space, and Artifacts

Turn back to the Unit 4 title page (page 85 in the Student's Book) and reread what it says about Chapter 8. Ask what *touch* and *space* mean. Point out that the term *artifacts* has a special definition here (clothing, jewelry, cars, houses, etc.), specific to the study of nonverbal communication. This definition of *artifacts* would not be included in a standard dictionary. Check for understanding of *channels of communication*. Ask, *What channels of communication did we hear discussed in the Chapter 7 interviews?* (eye contact, gestures, facial expressions, etc.) Have students look ahead in Chapter 8 to American Voices and locate the interviews with Marcos, SunRan, and Airi. Then have students locate the lecture on aspects of nonverbal communication (*Nonverbal Communication – The Hidden Dimension of Communication*).

---

1 GETTING STARTED *(pages 99–101)*

Discuss how the people in the drawing on page 99 in the Student's Book are communicating nonverbally.

Reading and thinking about the topic

1➤–3➤ After Step 1, elicit explanations of terms that students may not know, such as *subtle* and *largely*. Proceed with Steps 2 and 3.

Answers (page 99)

2➤ **1** communication via touch, space, and artifacts
    2 *Possible answers*:
      touch – shaking hands
      space – standing far away from someone you do not like
      artifacts – the jewelry you wear

Reading nonverbal cues

1➤–2➤ Before students begin Step 1, you might show some magazine ads that illustrate artifactual communication. Ask, *What kind of impression is this person trying to make by his/her choice of car/suit/haircut, etc.? What does he/she want people to think of him/her?* Then proceed with the task.

🎧 Listening to directions

1➤–2➤ Step 2 could also be done in pairs or small groups. Circulate and encourage discussion.

Answers (page 101)

1▶ *a* <u>5</u>   *b* <u>7</u>   *c* <u>3</u>   *d* <u>4</u>   *e* <u>8</u>   *f* <u>1</u>   *g* <u>2</u>   *h* <u>6</u>

---

2 AMERICAN VOICES: Marcos, SunRan, and Airi *(pages 102–105)*

If you have students from Brazil, Korea, or Japan, tell them to be ready to agree or disagree with what the interviewees say. Ask what category of nonverbal communication *clothing* falls under (artifactual). Call attention to the photograph of two male students in Benin holding hands on page 102 in the Student's Book. Ask whether this kind of touching is acceptable in students' culture(s).

BEFORE THE INTERVIEWS

Recalling what you already know

1▶–3▶ Before students begin Step 2, make sure they understand the chart's key. Encourage guessing. There are no absolute answers.

INTERVIEWS WITH MARCOS, SUNRAN, AND AIRI: Touch and space

As you read through the vocabulary box with students, demonstrate *backing up*.

🎧 Summarizing what you have heard

1▶–3▶ After Step 3, answer any questions about wording.

Sample answers (page 103)

1▶ Wording will vary. Alternatives are given in brackets.

> *Marcos*: Marcos was talking to a <u>student</u> of his from <u>Korea</u>. After a while he noticed that the student had <u>backed</u> into a <u>corner</u> because Marcos kept moving <u>toward him</u>. The student obviously felt very <u>uncomfortable</u>. Marcos had invaded his <u>body bubble [space]</u>.
>
> Marcos finds that he and his <u>wife</u> touch one another <u>less</u> here than they did in <u>Brazil</u>. Marcos also tries to stand <u>farther away</u> from people now that he lives in the United States.
>
> *SunRan*: SunRan has learned how to <u>shake hands</u> since she came here, but she has to remember <u>not to shake hands</u> when she visits <u>Korea</u>. She says that it is not good for <u>men</u> and <u>women</u> to <u>touch each other</u> in public in her country, but people of the same <u>sex</u> can hold <u>hands</u>. However, SunRan has to remember not to do that in the <u>United States</u>.

When she first came to the United States, SunRan was *shocked* by the fact that *high school kids* hug and *kiss* at school.

Airi: Airi says that Japanese people *never* hug and kiss one another. Her American husband felt *confused* by this at first: He thought his wife's family didn't *love him*. When Airi first came to the United States, she was *confused* at first because her American family *always hugged and kissed her*. But now she *likes it*.

INTERVIEW WITH AIRI: Clothing

Photographs of a *kimono*, a *cocktail dress*, and *bridesmaids' dresses* would be helpful.

🎧 *Listening for specific information*

1➤–3➤   After students read the statements in Step 1, encourage them to guess if the statements are about Japanese or American people based on their own knowledge of the two cultures. They should not write anything until Step 2.

Answers (page 104)

1➤   <u>A</u> *1*   <u>A</u> *4*   <u>J</u> *6*
　 <u>J</u> *2*   <u>J</u> *5*   <u>A</u> *7*
　 <u>A</u> *3*

AFTER THE INTERVIEWS

Personalizing the topic

Students may first discuss their answers in small groups before they do so as a class. If students are studying in the United States, have them compare changes in their own rules for touch and space in the class discussion.

Sharing your cultural perspective

Before starting the task, have American magazines available if at all possible. Alternatively, students could watch a short segment of an American movie or TV program, either as homework or in class.

Considering related information

1➤–2➤   After Step 1 check for understanding of the article excerpt.

Answers (page 105)

2➤   *1* in sports (*Answers to the second part of this question will vary.*)
　 2 *Possible answers*: They hug one another after wins or good plays. They slap hands, using their palms.
　 3 Winners are touched six times more often than losers. (*Answers to the second part of this question will vary.*)

3   IN YOUR OWN VOICE *(page 106)*

Review what constitutes *artifactual communication*.

Gathering data

1➤–2➤ Have students read Step 1. Then as a class think of other good places to observe the use of *touch*, *space*, or *artifacts*. See page 93 in the Student's Book for even more ideas. Have students share their findings in small groups and then as a class.

Using examples to illustrate a general point

Ask students if they can remember an example from this chapter that illustrates the idea of "body bubbles" (Marcos and his Korean student). Ask students if they find examples helpful, and if so, why.

1➤–5➤ Announce this task as "something completely different!" Have the following items available: magazines, scissors, paste or tape, and large pieces of construction or butcher paper. Read through Steps 1, 2, and 3 as a class. Answer any questions. This activity is fun, but that does not mean that it is not educational. It accomplishes three goals: (1) it allows students to demonstrate their understanding of artifactual communication by finding examples, (2) it gives them practice communicating and negotiating with others, and (3) it elicits a wide array of descriptive vocabulary.

Allow 40–50 minutes for Steps 1–3. As students work, circulate and help with language once they have found examples. (Do not tell them what qualities to look for.) Encourage everyone to participate in the search for examples, and in the defense of their choices. Tell students to find examples of at least six different nonverbal messages (sophistication, independence, innocence, etc.), and, if possible, more than one instance of each example. Be sure that students do not write words on their collages – only numbers. Their classmates will write what they think each number expresses on the corresponding blank sheet, posted in Step 4. Steps 4 and 5 could be done on the day after students do Steps 1–3.

4   ACADEMIC LISTENING AND NOTE TAKING: Nonverbal communication – the hidden dimension of communication *(pages 107–112)*

Ask students why they think nonverbal communication is being described as *hidden*. Check for understanding of *dimension* and *humor*.

BEFORE THE LECTURE

Recalling what you already know

1➤–3➤ Encourage students to note down any ideas they can think of from this chapter or from their own observations. For example, ask if they have noticed any differences in humor between people of different cultures. There are no right or wrong answers.

🎧 Note taking: Listening for stress and intonation

With students listening and following along, read the commentary box. Stop and check for comprehension as you read. Depending on their native language, students may find it very difficult to hear stress and/or intonation. Read the two example sentences (*That's my cousin . . .*) and ask students if they understand the difference. Demonstrate the two common patterns discussed (listing and contrast) with exaggerated stress and intonation.

1➤–3➤ In Step 1, all students should read aloud quietly to themselves. Do the same yourself to encourage students. After Step 1, ask for volunteers to say which pattern each sentence shows, and which words are being listed or contrasted. Proceed with Steps 2 and 3.

Answers (page 108)

1➤ **1** "How much is conveyed through verbal communication? More often than not, our intense emotions are conveyed nonverbally." (contrast)

2 "Most of our intense emotions are expressed through gestures, body position, facial expression, vocal cues, eye contact, use of space, and touching." (list)

3 "Imagine what would happen if you don't understand this bubble. What might you experience? Possibly discomfort, irritation, maybe even anger." (list)

4 "It could express affection, anger, playfulness, control, status – these are just a few functions of touch." (list)

5 "In some cultures it is common to see same-sex friends holding hands in public. However, think about this behavior in some other cultures. Is it appropriate?" (contrast)

LECTURE, Part One: Sarcasm and proxemics

Tell students that *sarcasm* and *proxemics* will be defined in the vocabulary exercise that follows.

Guessing vocabulary from context

1➤–2➤ Encourage students not to look at the definitions in Step 2 until they have told their partners as much as they can about the words in Step 1. Check matches as a class after Step 2.

Answers (page 109)

1➤
_c_ 1	_b_ 4	_d_ 6
_a_ 2	_g_ 5	_f_ 7
_e_ 3		

Summarizing what you have heard

1➤–4➤ After Step 1, answer any vocabulary questions. After Step 4, answer any questions about wording.

Sample answers (page 110)

1➤ Wording will vary. Alternatives are given in brackets.

NONVERBAL LANGUAGE – THE HIDDEN DIMENSION OF COMMUNICATION, Part One

Strong emotions are usually conveyed _nonverbally_: by gestures, body posture, _facial expression_, voice, eye contact, _space_, and _touching_.

Sometimes we rely completely on _nonverbal cues [gestures]_ to communicate. At other times nonverbal cues add to the meaning of the _words_ that we use. One good example of the second case is seen in our use of _humor_ and _sarcasm_. Often, in making a joke, Americans will say the opposite of what they mean. The only way to know what they really mean is to _observe [pay attention to, interpret]_ the _nonverbal_ cues that go along with their words. These could be their _tone of voice_ or a _facial_ expression.

An important area of _nonverbal_ communication is *proxemics*, the study of _personal space_. Each of us has a "_body bubble_" around us. Its size depends on several factors, such as _people's relationship_, the social context, and our _gender_. If someone enters our _bubble [personal space]_, we will _feel uncomfortable [tend to change our position]_. _Culture_ also plays an important role in proxemics; some cultures – for example, _Latin American [Middle Eastern]_ – have smaller bubbles than others.

LECTURE, Part Two: Touch

Guessing vocabulary from context

1➤–2➤ See the teacher's notes for *Guessing vocabulary from context* under LECTURE, Part One.

Answers (pages 110–111)

1➤

h	**1**
f	**2**
c	**3**
d	**4**
a	**5**
g	**6**
e	**7**
b	**8**

🎧 Summarizing what you have heard

1➤–4➤ See the teacher's notes for *Summarizing what you have heard* under LECTURE, Part One.

Sample answers (page 111)

1➤ Wording will vary. Alternatives are given in brackets.

NONVERBAL LANGUAGE – THE HIDDEN DIMENSION
OF COMMUNICATION, Part Two

Another important form of <u>*nonverbal communication*</u> is <u>*touch*</u>. As with space, rules of <u>*touch*</u> are very subtle, and they are mostly determined by <u>*gender*</u> and <u>*culture*</u>. What is acceptable in one culture may be <u>*taboo [unacceptable]*</u> in another culture. For example, in China, <u>*same-sex friends hold hands in public*</u>. But in the United States, <u>*this is taboo [this is interpreted as sexual]*</u>.

    In conclusion, we should remember that nonverbal <u>*misinterpretations [mistakes, misunderstandings]*</u> do not often result in cross-cultural <u>*anger [alienation]*</u>. In fact, these mistakes can be a source of <u>*humor [laughter]*</u> and <u>*camaraderie [friendship]*</u> between people of different cultures.

AFTER THE LECTURE

Sharing your personal and cultural perspective

Circulate and participate, and ask for a recap of each group's discussion of the questions when students have finished.

CHAPTER 8 Lecture Quiz

See the Lecture Quiz section at the back of this manual for a photocopiable quiz on the lecture for Chapter 8. Quiz answers can be found on pages 145–149.

Additional Ideas for Unit 4

1 Watch a short segment of an American film with the sound off. Choose one that shows typical American gestures, facial expressions, eye contact, and use of space and touching. See how much students can figure out about what is going on without the sound. You can also show films from other cultures (Japanese, Italian, French, etc.) and then look for cross-cultural differences in body language.

2 In a multicultural class, it can be interesting to observe two students from the same linguistic and cultural backgrounds conversing first in English and then in their own language. If you have students who are willing to do this, tell them to talk about anything that they normally would. Ask the class to observe their body language. Does it change in any way when they switch from their native language to English? Do they stand closer to each other or farther apart? What about eye contact?

3 A variation on the above activity can illustrate how we often say *maybe* and mean *no*, while at other times *maybe* means *yes*. I had two Japanese students role-play asking a slight acquaintance to go out for lunch – once with an acceptance and once with a refusal. The person responding used the same words each time, but indicated acceptance or refusal via tone of voice, facial expression, gestures, etc. I told the actors not to tell us in which order they were doing the two role-plays. The nonverbal signals were so subtle that the other Japanese students in the class were the only ones who could tell the difference. It would be interesting to try the same experiment with pairs of students from other cultures.

4 Have students stand up and talk to each other with space between them considered normal in American culture. Then have them move very slowly toward each other until they start to feel uncomfortable. Discuss reactions. Ask students to analyze how close they could get without feeling uncomfortable.

5 Bring in magazines from different countries and compare photographs of clothing, automobiles, architecture, jewelry, etc. Can students identify any clear cultural differences in artifactual communication?

6 Bring in a variety of cartoons from American magazines or newspapers. Are they funny across cultures?

UNIT 5
Interpersonal Relationships

UNIT TITLE PAGE

Read the unit title and ask students what *interpersonal* means. Elicit examples of interpersonal relationships (with friends, spouses, siblings, parents, children).

Read the unit summary paragraph with students and make sure that they understand all of the language. For example, what does it mean to *take friendships seriously*? Have students look ahead in Chapter 9 and locate the sections mentioned in the paragraph: the interview with the woman who takes her friendships seriously (Catherine) and the lecture on the meaning of friendship (*Looking at Friendship*).

CHAPTER 9
Friendship

1 GETTING STARTED (pages 114–115)

Reading and thinking about the topic

1➤–3➤ After Step 1, elicit or give explanations of terms that students may not know, such as *play a critical role*, *rhyme*, and *suffer*. Proceed with Steps 2 and 3.

Answers (pages 114–115)

2➤ **1** In childhood, it's important to have friends to play with. In adolescence, we spend a lot of time with our friends, and they give us support. In adulthood, we have less time and less need for friends, but they are still important.
  2 We have more time for friends, and we are going through a lot of physical and emotional changes; we need the support of friends.
  3 It is good to make new friends (silver), but old friends are even more valuable (gold).

Personalizing the topic

1➤–2➤ In Step 2, put the students in charge of figuring out the average length of time they have had the friends they named.

🎧 *Listening for specific information*

1▶–2▶ After Step 2, check answers as a class.

Answers (page 115)

1▶

Speaker	A good friend	When they met	Where they met
Otis	Hubert	27 years ago	in college
David	Odette	1985	in graduate school
Pam	Esther	1982	at synagogue
Tony	Tom	after WWII [1946]	at Yale
Catherine	Douglas	1968	in college
Ruth	Jeanette	1967	grade [elementary] school

---

2 AMERICAN VOICES: Catherine *(pages 116–118)*

BEFORE THE INTERVIEW

Recalling what you already know

1▶–2▶ There are no right or wrong answers to this task. Share ideas after Step 2 if time permits.

INTERVIEW WITH CATHERINE, Part One: Starting friendships

As students review the vocabulary box, show them a discreet *scar* if you have one. Ask how people get scars.

🎧 *Answering true/false questions*

1▶–3▶ Have volunteers give corrections of false statements to the class after Step 3.

Answers (page 117)

1▶
T	1
F	2
F	3
T	4
F	5

INTERVIEW WITH CATHERINE, Part Two: Maintaining friendships

Ask for an explanation of *maintain* as it is used in the title of this interview. When you get to *e-mail* in the vocabulary box, ask if any students use it, and if so, who they write to.

🎧 *Summarizing what you have heard*

1➤–3➤ After Step 3, answer questions about acceptable wording.

Sample answers (page 118)

1➤ Wording will vary. Alternatives are given in brackets.

> For Catherine, it's very important to <u>stay in touch with</u> [be current with] her friends. With some of her friends – for example, Odette – she stays in touch by <u>phone</u>. They talk <u>at least once a week</u>. Catherine also loves to <u>write letters</u>, and she never <u>throws them away</u>. As a result, she has a large collection of <u>letters</u> that forms a sort of <u>concrete record</u> of her life and of her friends' lives. She has been writing to her friend Doug for <u>about 20 years</u>. With some of her other friends, Catherine stays in touch by <u>e-mail</u>.
>
> According to Catherine, one of the most important things that friends can do for each other is <u>call each other on things</u> [let each other know if they're upset with them]. She believes that fighting is a way to show <u>that you care</u>. Other important things that friends give one another are comfort, <u>support</u>, <u>adventure</u>, and jokes. Finally, Catherine says that <u>friends</u> are "the family <u>we get to choose</u>."

AFTER THE INTERVIEW

Drawing inferences

Review what *inferences* are (see page 7 in the Student's Book).

Sample answers (page 118)

1 Some of the places where people first meet friends are <u>work and school</u>.
2 Friends are important because <u>they provide companionship, support, humor, and adventure, and they tell you when they think you are doing something wrong</u>.
3 In order to keep a friendship strong, you need to <u>stay in touch and be honest with each other</u>.

Sharing your personal and cultural perspective

If time permits, share answers to questions 2 and 3 as a class.

3   IN YOUR OWN VOICE *(page 119)*

Ask students to be thinking about a good friend that they would like to tell the class about.

Conducting a survey

1➤–3➤ Have students read through the task. Then answer students' questions. Review page 23 in the Student's Book for survey guidelines. Allow time for discussion of the presenters' findings.

Giving an oral presentation

1➤–2➤ Review guidelines for oral presentations on pages 8 and 39 in the Student's Book.

4   ACADEMIC LISTENING AND NOTE TAKING: Looking at friendship *(pages 120–125)*

Review what a *psychotherapist* is. Ask students to think about the topic *male/female differences in friendship* and ask if they can think of any differences between the genders.

BEFORE THE LECTURE

Building background knowledge on the topic: Culture notes

1➤ Bring in and play a recording of the song "People" by Barbra Streisand if possible.

2➤ After students read the excerpt, answer any vocabulary questions and then elicit the answers to the three comprehension questions. (The Anita Hill–Clarence Thomas controversy is tangential to the lecture: Mr. Rankin brings up the hearings to illustrate what he sees as an important difference in what men and women expect from their friends. However, it is worth familiarizing students with the event because it will help them follow the lecture.)

Answers *(page 120)*

2➤ *1* He is a U.S. Supreme Court judge.
2 Anita Hill, a law professor, testified at the hearing. She had worked with Thomas during the 1980s, and she testified that Thomas had sexually harassed her at work.
3 The hearings were on television.

🎧 *Note taking: Using morphology, context, and nonverbal cues to guess word meaning*

With students listening and following along, read the commentary box. Stop and check for comprehension as you read. Ask students for examples of morphological clues. For example, ask the following questions: *If a word ends in* -ment, *what can we guess about it?* (It's a noun.) *What can we guess about the meaning of a word like* malignant? (It probably means something bad because *mal-* = bad.) Underscore the point in the last paragraph: Partial understanding of a word is often sufficient for comprehension of a lecture.

1▶–3▶ Before students begin the task, tell them that the purpose here is to work on their guessing skills. No dictionaries allowed! In Step 3, allow students to conduct the activity.

Sample answers (page 121)

1▶ **1** subjective: *meaning different things to different people*

2 social network, or support systems: *family and friends*

3 loners: *people who are always alone, who prefer to be alone* (morphology)

4 vulnerable: *at risk, afraid of (rejection)*

5 incredulous: *unable to believe, very surprised* (morphology)

LECTURE, Part One: The role of friendship in psychotherapy

Ask students what they expect to hear about in this part of the lecture.

Guessing vocabulary from context

1▶–2▶ Encourage students not to look at the definitions in Step 2 until they have told their partners as much as they can about the words in Step 1. Check matches as a class after Step 2.

Answers (page 122)

1▶

c	**1**
f	**2**
l	**3**
d	**4**
h	**5**
g	**6**
i	**7**
j	**8**
b	**9**
a	**10**
k	**11**
e	**12**

🎧 Listening for specific information

1➤–3➤ As in Chapter 6, this task can be used either as a quiz or as an ordinary listening task in which students are given the questions beforehand. If you would like to treat this task as a quiz, you may want to photocopy page 159 at the back of this book and then collect these sheets after students have completed the listening task. Review answers as a class after Step 3.

Sample answers (page 123)

1➤ Wording will vary.

1 A song titled "People" caused the lecturer to think about friendship. The song says that people who need other people are lucky.
2 Social networks are an important sign of how a person is getting along. A person needs to feel supported by family and friends.
3 Clients who have support systems are much less likely to commit suicide, and if clients are feeling suicidal, it is important for their friends and family to know it.
4 Friends may reject us.
5 They are afraid of – or tired of – being rejected. It's less painful to simply be a loner.

LECTURE, Part Two: How male and female friendships differ

Ask students if they have thought of any more differences between male and female friendships.

Guessing vocabulary from context

1➤–2➤ See the teacher's notes for *Guessing vocabulary from context* under LECTURE, Part One.

Answers (page 123)

1➤
b	**1**
d	**2**
f	**3**
c	**4**
a	**5**
e	**6**

🎧 Listening for specific information

1➤–3➤ See the teacher's notes for *Listening for specific information* under LECTURE, Part One. If you would like to treat this task as a quiz, you may want to photocopy page 159 at the back of this book.

Sample answers (page 124)

1➤ Wording will vary.

1 In general, women enjoy talking about their lives and about their feelings. Men generally prefer doing things together rather than talking.

2 Women want to be listened to and comforted. Men want to solve their friends' problems or have their friends solve their problems.

3 Anita Hill testified that Clarence Thomas had sexually harassed her while they were working together in the 1980s and that she had spoken to several of her colleagues about it at the time.

4 Anita Hill's colleagues (all female) did not give her advice; they simply listened to her. But the male senators who questioned Hill's colleagues could not believe that her friends would not have advised her, and many concluded that she had not told them at all.

5 We need to be loved and accepted for who we are.

AFTER THE LECTURE

Sharing your personal perspective

1➤–4➤ Take time for the class to share what they discussed in pairs or small groups.

Considering related information

1➤–2➤ After Step 1, check for understanding of the excerpt. After Step 2, let small groups share what they discussed with the rest of the class.

Answers (page 125)

2➤ *1* Males like to do things together. "The third thing" is an activity or task of some sort.

2 Yes, the lecturer made the point that males in general prefer to do something together rather than to talk.

Answers to questions 3 and 4 will vary.

CHAPTER 9 Lecture Quiz

See the Lecture Quiz section at the back of this manual for a photocopiable quiz on the lecture for Chapter 9. Quiz answers can be found on pages 145–149.

Love

Turn back to the Unit 5 title page (page 113 in the Student's Book) and reread what it says about Chapter 10. Have students look ahead in Chapter 10 to American Voices and locate the interview with a happily married couple (Ann and Jim). Then have students locate the lecture on love (*Love – What's It All About?*). Ask for a synonym for *fall in love*.

1 GETTING STARTED *(pages 126–128)*

Check for understanding of *to last* and *matchmaker*.

Reading and thinking about the topic

1➤–3➤ After Step 1, elicit explanations of terms that students may not know, such as *complement*, *outgoing*, and *issues*. Proceed with Steps 2 and 3.

Answers *(pages 126–127)*

2➤ **1** *Answers will vary.* The first question refers to initial attraction, and the second refers to long-term commitment.
2 One person may be shy and the other outgoing.
3 They have similar backgrounds, values, opinions, and interests.

Personalizing the topic

1➤–4➤ Have students read through the chart in Step 2. Then answer any vocabulary questions that students have. Proceed with the task. Participate yourself. Let students share their responses to the question in Step 4 as a class, if they like.

🎧 Listening for details

Remind students that when they are trying to take down as much information as possible, they should use abbreviations and symbols.

1➤–4➤ While students are doing Step 3, circulate and listen. In Step 4, ask whether students paired couples who *match* one another or *complement* one another. After students complete the task, draw their attention to the cartoon on page 128 in the Student's Book. Ask, *Do the two people match or complement each other?*

Sample answers *(page 128)*

1➤ These are sample notes.

1 Les: librarian, divorced, late 30s, likes jazz, movies, museums, wants a match

2 Michael: M.D., works hard, climbs mts., 35, wants attractive, younger wm.

3 Alicia: wants kind, depend. man, gd. father; has 2 chldrn. (4 & 6), comput. engin.

4 Frank: Jr. HS tchr., likes garden'g., baseball, 37

5 Sara: artist, early 40s, shy, likes to talk abt. art & books

6 Suzanne: into health, mid 20s, wants mature man, rich

---

2 AMERICAN VOICES: Ann and Jim *(pages 129–132)*

BEFORE THE INTERVIEW

Sharing your cultural perspective

1➤–*2*➤ After Step 2, share answers as a class.

INTERVIEW WITH ANN AND JIM, Part One: Courtship

Read the vocabulary items in the box aloud. Answer any questions.

🎧 *Listening for specific information*

1➤–*3*➤ After Step 1, answer any questions about vocabulary. Proceed with the task.

Answers (page 130)

1➤ *1* 31 years
  2 Ann was a senior in high school (16) and Jim was a senior in college.
  3 She thought he was the best person she had ever met.
  4 She was afraid that Jim would marry her older sister.
  5 11 years
  6 A friend warned him that Ann was thinking of marrying someone else, so he drove to her home and asked her mother for permission to marry Ann.
  7 She feels fortunate that she didn't give up and marry someone else during the 11 years that it took Jim to propose.

INTERVIEW WITH ANN AND JIM, Part Two: Making marriage work

Bring in a photo album, if possible, to help students understand the meaning of *album* as it is defined in the vocabulary box.

🎧 *Listening for specific information*

1➤–*3*➤ See the teacher's notes for *Listening for specific information* under INTERVIEW WITH ANN AND JIM, Part One.

Answers (page 131)

1➤ **1** They have both done interesting things in their lives, and they are proud of one another's accomplishments.
2 classical music, living in other countries and learning about other cultures, gardening, walking, family, church
3 Ann is good at financial management and keeping records, and Jim is not.
4 They respect each other.
5 working overseas, living in a tent in the Somalian desert for three months, raising their two boys: These experiences have been sometimes difficult, but they have bonded Ann and Jim.

AFTER THE INTERVIEW

Sharing your personal and cultural perspective

Circulate and participate. After students have discussed the questions, share answers as a class.

Considering related information

1➤–4➤ For Step 2, students choose to be either A or B. B students should turn their books upside down and look only at their own table. Put students in charge of writing information on the board in Steps 3 and 4.

Sample answers (page 132)

3➤ When first meeting someone of the opposite sex, . . .
- men and women are equally likely to notice height and hair.
- women are more likely to notice clothing, eyes, and smile.
- very few men or women notice hands.
- men are more than twelve times as likely to notice legs.
- men are more than 1 1/2 times more apt to notice figures.
- women are less than half as likely as men to notice teeth.

3   IN YOUR OWN VOICE (page 133)

Ask students to start thinking about whom they could interview.

Conducting a survey

1➤–4➤ Have students read through the task. Then circulate and offer help with Steps 1 and 2. Review page 23 in the Student's Book for more details.

Gathering data

1➤–3➤ Have students read through the task. If they are having trouble thinking of questions to ask, brainstorm as a class. If an English-speaking couple is unavailable, students may interview a couple in their first language and then translate their information into English for the class.

---

4   ACADEMIC LISTENING AND NOTE TAKING: Love – What's it all about? *(pages 134–139)*

BEFORE THE LECTURE

Building background knowledge on the topic

1➤–2➤ After Step 2, share answers as a class. Do not provide answers yourself.

Sample answers (page 134)

2➤ *1* "The matching hypothesis" probably looks for the ways that couples are alike.
2 Possible answers: age, interests, ethnic background
3 If two people *complement* each other, it means that their differences have a positive effect on their relationship.
4 Romeo and Juliet come from families that hate each other. They meet, fall in love, and marry secretly. But Romeo is forced to kill Juliet's cousin in a fight. Both Romeo and Juliet die at the end of the story. Romeo kills himself because he thinks that Juliet is dead, and Juliet kills herself when she sees that Romeo has killed himself.
5 People are interested in people whom their parents oppose.

⌢ *Note taking: Taking advantage of rhetorical questions*

With students listening and following along, read the commentary box. Stop and check for comprehension as you read. Ask students if professors in their country use rhetorical questions. Ask if there is student participation during lectures.

1➤–2➤ Turn off the tape after each rhetorical question in Step 1. Point out that students do *not* need to write the questions – only the answers that they expect to hear. Give students plenty of time for the first question. After they write, restart the tape, giving slightly less time as you proceed with the next five questions. After students have heard all the questions and written what they expect to hear after each, have them reconstruct the questions with a partner and compare predicted answers. In Step 2, the same questions – this time followed by answers – are heard without interruption.

Answers (page 135)

1➤ Here are the questions the students will hear in Step 1, and sample predictions:

1 *Rhetorical question*: Why do you fall in love with one person, but not another person?
   Predicted answer: An explanation or theory of why one person falls in love with another person.

2 *Rhetorical question*: A lot of people might like a ten, but if you're a five, then who are you going to end up getting married to?
   Predicted answer: A person who is a five will most likely end up with a five.

3 *Rhetorical question*: If she graduated from graduate school, and he flunked out of kindergarten, do you think that relationship is going to last very long?
   Predicted answer: No, a relationship between a highly educated person and a person with no education probably will not last long.

4 *Rhetorical question*: You'd have the same age, or about. What's the accepted age range?
   Predicted answer: The biggest acceptable difference in age between a husband and wife.

5 *Rhetorical question*: Now, what about the idea that opposites attract?
   Predicted answer: A comment about or explanation of the idea that opposites attract.

6 *Rhetorical question*: You know that story of Romeo and Juliet?
   Predicted answer: An explanation of the story of Romeo and Juliet.

2➤ Here are the actual answers to the rhetorical questions, which students will hear in Step 2:

   1 The sociobiology people would tend to say you fall in love – unconsciously – with somebody that's a good genetic match.
   2 probably somebody closer to a five
   3 probably not
   4 usually 5 to 10 years
   5 You've probably heard that, that's the *complementary* theory, or *complementarity*.
   6 Uhh, their families *hated* each other, and they said, "You stay away from him!" "You stay away from her!"

LECTURE, Part One: The matching hypothesis

Elicit students' guesses about the meaning of *the matching hypothesis*.

Guessing vocabulary from context

1➤–2➤ Encourage students not to look at the definitions in Step 2 until they have told their partners as much as they can about the words in Step 1. Check matches as a class after Step 2.

Answers (page 136)

1➤
d	**1**
g	**2**
h	**3**
i	**4**
e	**5**
c	**6**
f	**7**
a	**8**
j	**9**
b	**10**

🎧 Outlining practice

1➤–4➤ After Step 1, get students to say as much as they can about the structure and content of Part One of the lecture. After Step 4, check answers as a class.

Sample answers (page 137)

1➤ Some wording will vary.

LOVE – WHAT'S IT ALL ABOUT? Part One

I. the matching hypothesis = *we tend to be attracted to people who are like us*
   A. possible areas of similarity
      1. physical
         e.g., *a "five" is probably going to marry a "five," not a "ten"*
      2. personality
      3. *job*
      4. *similar intelligence*
      5. education
         e.g., *college graduate who marries hs grad. – problems – too big a gap*
      6. same interests
      7. *same values*
      8. *religion*
      9. race
     10. age: *usually within 5–10 years*
     11. *socio-economic status*

LECTURE, Part Two: The matching hypothesis (continued) and other theories

Guessing vocabulary from context

1➤–2➤ See the teacher's notes for *Guessing vocabulary from context* under LECTURE, Part One. Point out the cartoon on page 138 in the Student's Book. See if a student can explain it. Ask if this is an example of *matching* or *complementarity*.

Answers (page 137)

1▶

b	**1**
d	**2**
c	**3**
a	**4**
f	**5**
e	**6**

🎧 *Outlining practice*

1▶–4▶ See the teacher's notes for *Outlining practice* under LECTURE, Part One.

Sample answers (page 138)

1▶ Some wording will vary.

LOVE – WHAT'S IT ALL ABOUT? Part Two

I. (cont.) The matching hypothesis, general rule: *the ↑ similar you are, the ↑ likely to stay married.*
   A. possible areas of similarity (cont.)
      12. *politics – want pers. who validates our ideas*
II. Complementarity = the idea that opposites attract – sometimes works in rel'ships
   e.g., *submissive pers. is happier with a dominant pers. than w/ another sub. pers.*
III. The Romeo and Juliet effect = *more oppos. from parents, etc. → more attraction*
IV. Conclusion: *most import't idea = similarity – we are attracted to people like us*

AFTER THE LECTURE

Applying general concepts to specific data

Do questions 1 and 2 separately. Check for understanding of each question before having students discuss in pairs or small groups, and allow time after each question for them to hear their classmates' ideas.

Sharing your personal and cultural perspective

1▶–4▶ Circulate and participate as students discuss the questions.

CHAPTER 10 Lecture Quiz

See the Lecture Quiz section at the back of this manual for a photocopiable quiz on the lecture for Chapter 10. Quiz answers can be found on pages 145–149.

Additional Ideas for Unit 5

1 There are many good movies that depict friendship or love. Such films can be used as a springboard for a discussion of some of the topics brought up in this unit. Here are some examples:

- *When Harry Met Sally*, with Meg Ryan and Billy Crystal, shows a friendship that develops into love. Watch it and discuss why the two main characters are attracted to each other. Do they complement each other? Do they match?
- *Beaches*, starring Bette Midler and Barbara Hershey, is about a lifelong friendship between two women.
- *Stand By Me*, starring River Phoenix, is the story of four boys who take a trip together that changes their lives.
- *City Slickers*, starring Billy Crystal, is the story of three male friends who have a cowboy adventure together.

2 The ideas on page 133 in the Student's Book, *Conducting a survey*, Step 1, could also work as debate topics.

3 If available, bring in personal advertisements from a local newspaper. Most personal ads use a great many abbreviations, so be sure to provide a key, or have students construct one with your help. Locate ads from people seeking friendship, love, marriage, etc. Have students play matchmaker. Or create a matching role-play activity: Paste ads to note cards and have each student pick one at random; then tell students to circulate and look for a good match by asking for and giving personal information based on the ad they chose. A less risky alternative would be a concentration-style game, with matches on 3- x 5-inch note cards, placed upside down on a table. Students turn over two cards with personal ads pasted to them. If they think the two people who wrote the ads would make a good couple, they have to justify their reasoning to the other players.

LISTENING SCRIPT

Listening Script

Narrator: *Academic Listening Encounters: Listening, Note Taking, and Discussion* by Miriam Espeseth.
Series editor: Bernard Seal.
Content focus: Human Behavior.
Published by Cambridge University Press.
These cassettes contain the listening material for the *Academic Listening Encounters: Listening, Note Taking, and Discussion* Student's Book.
This recording is copyright.

Narrator: Cassette 1.
Chapter 1, The Influence of Mind Over Body
Page 3
Listening to directions, Step 1

Woman: Modern life is stressful. Many of us walk around all day with tight muscles in our necks, our chests, our backs. It's not surprising that we get headaches, and feel tired, and sometimes even make ourselves physically ill. But just as our minds can make our bodies feel more *stressed*, our minds can also help us relax. We're now going to do a relaxation exercise called "mind over matter." The expression "mind over matter" simply means that your mind is very powerful, and it can control your physical state. In this relaxation exercise, your mind is going to tell your body how to feel. And your body will listen to your mind, and it will become deeply, deeply relaxed.

First, sit comfortably. Now, close your eyes and take a couple of deep breaths. Breathe in slowly and deeply through your nose. Then, breathe out slowly through your mouth. Keep your eyes closed. As you breathe, repeat these words in your mind: *I am feeling very peaceful and quiet. I am feeling very peaceful and quiet.* Keep your eyes closed and continue to breathe gently, but normally. Relax your shoulders and let the air push your stomach out as you breathe in.

Now focus on your left arm. Think about nothing but your left arm, and say these words in your mind: *My left arm feels warm and heavy.* Keep saying it to yourself: *My left arm feels warm and heavy.* Soon your left arm will begin to feel warm and very, very heavy. Feel that now.

Continue to breathe quietly and gently, with your eyes closed. Now focus on your right arm. Tell yourself that it feels warm and heavy. Warm and heavy. Warm and heavy. Now your left leg: *My left leg feels warm and heavy.* Now your right leg. Now take one last deep breath and stretch. Open your eyes and pay attention to how you feel. Your body should feel much more relaxed and your mind should feel clear.

Narrator: Now complete the steps in your book.

Narrator: Chapter 1, The Influence of Mind Over Body
Page 5
Personalizing the topic, Step 2

Interviewer: Nancy, how long have you been teaching?
Nancy: Mmm, let's see, I've been teaching for twenty years now.
Interviewer: Twenty years!
Nancy: Yeah.

Interviewer: And have you always taught first grade?

Nancy: No, actually I've taught a variety of ages of children. Uh, I taught three-year-olds and preschool children for seven years, and then I taught fifth, fourth, and first grade at the elementary level.

Interviewer: So, always children.

Nancy: That's right.

Interviewer: Now, would you say that being an elementary school teacher was a stressful job?

Nancy: Yes, very much so.

Interviewer: And what is stressful about it?

Nancy: Well, the children bring a lot of problems into the classroom – problems from home, and then there are developmental things going on with each age, too – emotional and social, uh–

Interviewer: Could you think of, uh, an example of something stressful that happens at school? Y'know, something typical.

Nancy: Well, I guess when I'm trying to teach something new to a class of five- and six-year-olds, and that's about thirty-two students now, and you're trying to teach a new concept, and there's one disruptive child, and a lot of times lately there's been *more* than one disruptive child at a time who can't pay attention and is disturbing the children around him. So it pulls everyone off track.

Interviewer: So that you can't teach the lesson.

Nancy: Right. As a teacher you feel it's your job to be teaching these things that are in the curriculum, and then you end up spending so much time trying to teach children how to get along in the classroom setting – and how to behave, and be polite to each other – and it seems like there gets to be less and less time to teach what we're supposed to be teaching.

Interviewer: OK, so there's less time for teaching and more time spent on–

Nancy: On helping children work out their personal problems.

Interviewer: Hmm. Now, Nancy, you say that teaching is very stressful. Do you think it's *more* stressful than *other* kinds of work? Have you had other jobs besides teaching that were–

Nancy: Yes, I've done office work and sales, and the big difference with teaching is that you're never really finished! I mean, when I did those other jobs, I could go home at five or whatever and forget about it till the next morning. But with teaching, it's never over until summer vacation.

Interviewer: Uh-huh.

Nancy: Y'know, I mean you carry around the responsibility of those children all the time.

Interviewer: So, evenings and weekends–

Nancy: Uh-huh, you are never really free of the stress of, of that *responsibility*.

Interviewer: Hmm. How does that stress manifest itself?

Nancy: *Fatigue!*

Interviewer: Fatigue. You feel tired a lot?

Nancy: Yeah. I think that comes with working with young children. And the younger the child you work with, the more energy they require. I think any mother of a young child will tell you that.

Interviewer: So you feel tired. Anything else? Do you ever lose your temper?

Nancy: Well, I have to *keep* my temper in the classroom. I mean, that's my job. But I do find that, um, now that I have a child of my own, I sometimes have less patience with him. And it's probably related to the fact that I've spent the whole day being very patient with *thirty-two* children! I mean, I have to admit that I'm a much better mother during the summer than I am during the school year.

Interviewer: Nancy, do you find that as a teacher you get sick more often than other people?

Nancy: Definitely! Especially when I was teaching preschool. Whatever cold or flu the children got, I would get, too.

Interviewer: Because of the stress of working with little kids? Or–

Nancy: Partly, yeah. I really believe that stress *does* make you more susceptible to illness, that it weakens your immune system.

Interviewer: Mmm.

Nancy: But I also think that the smaller the child, the closer you work with him, I mean, physically. I mean, y'know, the kids're *in your lap*, in your *face*, and they're *coughing*, *sneezing*, and touching you, and maybe your tolerance would be higher if you weren't under so much stress. I think it's related.

Interviewer: Hmm. Nancy, what do you do to *relieve* stress?

Nancy: Well, I find it's very important to exercise. I, I go to an exercise class regularly.

Interviewer: Mhhm.

Nancy: Mhhm. And also it's been very important to me to have good friends that I can talk to when I need to.

Narrator: Now complete the steps in your book.

Narrator: Chapter 1, The Influence of Mind Over Body
Page 5
Listening for specific information, Step 2, Page 6

[Entire interview with Nancy is repeated.]

Narrator: Now complete the steps in your book.

Narrator: Chapter 1, The Influence of Mind Over Body
Page 6
Listening for specific information, Step 2

Interviewer: Sam, how long have you been a police officer?

Sam: I've been a police officer for twenty-five years.

Interviewer: Twenty-five years. And you've had different types of assignments on the police force?

Sam: Yeah, I've done everything from patrol to undercover work to detective work, and now I'm supervising investigations.

Interviewer: Sam, I think most people would say that being a police officer is a very *stressful* job. Would you agree?

Sam: Yes, it's *definitely* a stressful job.

Interviewer: OK.

Sam: But of course it depends on your assignment.

Interviewer: So, what's probably the most stressful assignment you can have?

Sam: Uh, I'd say patrol is the most stressful assignment.

Interviewer: Interesting! In what way?

Sam: Well, I guess the biggest part of the stress is the fear factor – the fear of the unknown. In patrol work, you don't know from moment to moment who you are talking to or what their reaction is going to be to just your *presence*.

Interviewer: Hmm.

Sam: Let's say, for example, a patrol officer stops someone for a traffic violation. Now, it would seem as though that would be a very *low*-stress situation. But the truth is, there are more police officers stopped – pardon me – *injured* during a routine stop like that than in any other facet of police work.

Interviewer: Really?

Sam: Really! All police officers are taught from the very beginning that *that* is a time when they *must* be aware of their surroundings, of what the person in the car is *doing*, because they could be *dead* before they get back to their car. People back *over* policemen, people *shoot* policemen, people *jump out* at policemen – different things. So that's probably the most stressful time.

Interviewer: I see. Sam, there's some research to suggest that there's a connection between stress and illness. Do you think that there's a higher percentage of illness among police officers than in the general population? I mean, do they get more colds or anything? Is this really true?

Sam: Yes, it is, and the stress level not only manifests itself, um, in daily health – whether or not you're feeling well on any given day. It also manifests itself in things like ulcers, heart disease – police officers tend to have a higher rate of heart disease and ulcers than people in other professions.

Interviewer: Really? That's documented?

Sam: Yes, it's documented. And also the *divorce* rate among police officers is much higher.

Interviewer: Really? Is there something that the police department *does* to help you deal with this stress?

Sam: Yes, there are several programs that most police departments have in place. One is a physical training or exercise program – an established program where some part of your day is spent on some type of physical exercise. They've found that that's a great stress reducer. Um, there's also a psychological program with counseling for officers to help them reduce their stress. And there are several discussion groups. They've found that sometimes just sitting around and *talking* about the stress – with other officers – helps to reduce it. So, those things are available.

Interviewer: And what do *you* do, *personally*, to help you deal with the stress of your job?

Sam: Well, during the baseball season, I'm the biggest baseball *fanatic*, and I will either be *reading* about baseball, or *listening* to baseball, or *watching* baseball. Another thing I try to do is to get some sort of exercise every day. And then, I work hard at keeping my personal relationships, especially my relationship with my wife, at its peak. I'm very fortunate that I have a good relationship with my wife, and a *good* marriage. So when I come home, I can talk about my day with her, and then just forget about it.

Narrator: Now complete the steps in your book.

Narrator: Chapter 1, The Influence of Mind Over Body
Page 10
Note taking: Using telegraphic language, Step 2

Narrator: One.

Lecturer: Um, think of people that you know with migraine headaches, or high blood pressure, skin rashes, ulcers, high cholesterol, heart disease, uh, the list goes on and on. All of these symptoms may be related to psychosomatic disorders or disorders where there is a *physical* symptom that's caused by a *psychological* problem.

Narrator: Two.

Lecturer: We have found through recent research that the *efficiency* of the immune system is compromised, damaged, by certain stressors, and we have, um, support for this from *two* areas of research – both from humans and from animals.

Narrator: Three.

Lecturer: More and more health care professionals are responding to this research, and agreeing that the mind can have a powerful effect on the body, and that this effect is *especially* negative when a patient feels helpless, feels he has no control.

Narrator: Four.

Lecturer: In the case of problems like headaches, sleeplessness, um, even high blood pressure, more and more health care providers are teaching patients to control these by simple relaxation techniques, which can be very effective – more effective than medication.

Narrator: Now complete the steps in your book.

Narrator: Chapter 1, The Influence of Mind Over Body
Page 12
Summarizing what you have heard, Step 2

Lecturer: It seems obvious that the mind will have an effect on the body, but we're now just coming to the realization and gathering some hard data that that is *true*, that the way that you think actually affects the way that your body feels. Uh, stress has real implications, uh, for, um, in terms of what it can do to the body, and psychosomatic disorders, or disorders where there is a physical symptom that's caused by a psychological problem, is a real hot topic in psychology today because it's, it's the border between psychology and medicine and relevant to almost all of our lives. Think of people that you know with migraine headaches or high blood pressure, skin rashes, ulcers, high cholesterol, heart disease. Um, the list goes on and on. All of these symptoms may be related to psychosomatic disorders.

What I want to focus on today is a new area of research on stress and illness, and this new field is called *psychoneuroimmunology*, or *PNI* for abbreviation. I suggest that you start abbreviating it. The word *psycho neuro immunology*: *psycho* means, um, the mind, the way that a person thinks; *neuro* is the nervous system; and *immunology* is the body's defense against disease, the immune system.

The immune system has two important tasks: um, basically to recognize foreign invaders, things that, that come into the body, um, and then to inactivate them and remove them from the body. Uh, we have found through recent research that the efficiency of the immune system is compromised, damaged, by certain stressors, and we have support for this from two areas of research – both from humans and from animals.

And I'll start with some of the animal studies: We know that, uh, rats or mice that are placed in a situation where there was uncontrollable or unpredictable stress, uh – for example, shining bright lights on them or giving electrical shocks to their, their feet or overcrowding them, which, y'know, would be stressful – when these rats are infected with cancer cells and then placed in an environment like these, they're much more likely to develop cancer under these stressful conditions than if they're in *nonstressful* conditions.

Another really important study done with animals and immune functioning was done by, um, a fellow named Robert Ader. Ader was actually doing a study on *taste* aversion in rats when he discovered, quite by accident, that he was able to condition the rats' immune systems to malfunction. Now, this has very powerful implications because if we can teach the immune system to, uh, if, if we can condition it to *malfunction*, then it makes sense that we could also condition it to get better and to heal itself without medicine, and that's very exciting. That's where we are now, in, uh, in this research.

Narrator: Now complete the steps in your book.

Narrator: **Chapter 1, The Influence of Mind Over Body**
Page 13
Summarizing what you have heard, Step 2

Lecturer: And some of the, um, studies on *humans* also support this idea that the mind can control the immune system. We know that, uh, we know that people under great stress – when we analyze some of their immune functioning – we know that right *before* they experience a stressor, uh, their immune systems become compromised – for example, accountants before tax time and students before final exams. So if you think in terms of classical conditioning, y'know, uh, like Pavlov and his experiments with dogs, uh, in *our* case the mental stress of just *thinking* about the exam or just *thinking* about being very busy at work is acting like, uh, acting like Pavlov's bell – acting as a conditioned stimulus to depress the immune system.

We're finding that today in the medical field more and more health care professionals are responding to this research and agreeing that the mind can have a powerful effect on the body, and that this effect is *especially* negative when a patient feels helpless, feels he has no control. Um, elderly people in nursing homes. We know that, uh, there was one study done on nursing home residents: one group of elderly people who felt that they were in control of their lives and made the choice to be there; another group that was, uh, that felt that they were placed there by their family members, and who really didn't want to be there and felt out of control of the decision. And the, the ones who felt *out* of control were much more likely to get sick and to *die*, to lead unhealthy lives, while the ones who felt *in* control tended to be healthier.

And, uh, another way in which the mind can exert a *positive* influence on the body is in the case of problems like headaches, sleeplessness, uh, even high blood pressure. Um, more and more health care providers are teaching patients to control these by simple relaxation techniques, which can be very effective – more effective than medication. So, there's, um, real exciting implications with this work that, uh, we're getting closer to understanding how powerful the mind is in controlling the body.

Narrator: Now complete the steps in your book. This is the end of Chapter 1. Now please turn over the cassette to continue.

2

Narrator: Chapter 2, Preventing Illness
Page 16
Listening to directions, Step 1

Man: In this exercise you are going to measure your heart rate, that is, how many times per minute your heart beats. It's very easy to measure your heart rate. You can feel it at several points on your body, for example, on your wrists or on either side of your neck. What you are feeling is called your *pulse*. What exactly is happening when we feel our pulse?

When the heart beats, there is a short pause after each beat. During this pause, the blood is pushed through the arteries in our body. This movement of blood causes a kind of wave. And we can feel this wave at the points where arteries are close to the surface of the skin.

We all know that our hearts beat faster when we are working hard physically. The reason for this is that our muscles need more oxygen in order to work, and oxygen is carried in the blood.

Now let's see how our heart rates respond to the needs of our muscles. Sit quietly and relax. Just breathe normally in and out. Take your right hand and, with the first two fingers, feel the side of your neck until you locate your pulse. Can you find it? Just keep your fingers resting lightly on your pulse. We're going to measure it for fifteen seconds. When I say *go*, begin counting. Begin with zero, not one. Keep counting your pulse until I say *stop*. Are you ready? Go!

Stop. Now multiply the number of beats that you counted by four. That is your resting heart rate. Write it down in your book where it says *first heart rate*.

Now we're going to see what effect a little exercise will have on your heart rate. I'm going to ask you to stand up and do some movements with your arms – first your right arm, then your left, then both – either up, forward (that is, in front of you), or to the side. After each movement, bring your arms back to your sides. Be sure that you have enough room to put your arms out to the side without hitting your classmates. Now I want you to use a lot of energy. Really move those arms. OK? Are you ready? Right arm first. Here we go.

Right arm **up**, now left arm **up**, now both arms **up**.
Again right arm **up**, now left arm **up**, now both arms **up**.

Now forward **right**, forward **left**, both **forward**.
Again forward **right**, forward **left**, both **forward**.
Now to the side **right**, to the side **left**, to the side **both**.
Again to the side **right**, to the side **left**, to the side **both**.
Now both arms **up**, again **up**, again **up**.
Again both arms **up**, again **up**, again **up**.
Now both arms **forward**, again **forward**, again **forward**.
Again both arms **forward**, again **forward**, again **forward**.
Now to the **side**, again **side**, again **side**.
Again to the **side**, again **side**, again **side**, and **stop**.

Good work! Find your pulse on the side of your neck and let's get ready to count beginning with zero. Ready? Go!
Stop. Now multiply by four, and write down your *second* heart rate in your book. Subtract and find your increase.

Narrator: Now complete the steps in your book.

Narrator: Chapter 2, Preventing Illness
Page 18
Restating what you have heard, Step 2

Interviewer: Pat, I understand that you used to smoke. Is that right?
Pat: Yes, *heavily*.
Interviewer: How heavily?
Pat: I started when I was probably, what, thirteen, fourteen.
Interviewer: Hmm!
Pat: And I smoked for about, um, twenty years on cigarettes and then I switched to a pipe and smoked a pipe for about, uh, five years.
Interviewer: And, uh, why did you start smoking in the first place? That's kind of young.
Pat: It was cool.
Interviewer: Were your friends smoking?

Pat: Yeah, you know, peer pressure, that kind of–
Interviewer: What did your parents say?
Pat: Oh, they tried to make me quit from time to time, but it never did any good.
Interviewer: Uh-huh. Now how much, how much did you smoke? How many cigarettes a day?
Pat: Um, at the peak, twenty to thirty – a pack and a half.
Interviewer: So, now, you started when you were about thirteen and you smoked for twenty-five years, did you say?
Pat: Right.
Interviewer: Twenty-five years. And, uh, did you ever try to quit?
Pat: Oh, yes. I tried several times.
Interviewer: What method did you use to try to quit?
Pat: Just willpower.
Interviewer: Did you ever succeed for a short time?
Pat: Oh, for *days* at a time.
Interviewer: Hmm.
Pat: Well, my senior year in high school, I played basketball, and my coach convinced me that I'd play better if I quit smoking, so I quit smoking for the season.
Interviewer: Hmm!
Pat: And the day after we lost our last game I, uh, started up again.
Interviewer: Back to the cigarettes, huh?
Pat: Yeah.
Interviewer: Well, uh, so when did you finally quit?
Pat: Uh, when was that? About, um, 1983, I think.
Interviewer: 1983?
Pat: Right. I had a heart attack and they wouldn't let me smoke in the hospital.
Interviewer: A *heart attack*?! Was it a bad one?
Pat: No, it was fairly mild, but it was enough to scare me.
Interviewer: I can imagine.
Pat: And, then while I was in the hospital, my wife threw away all my tobacco and pipes and, by the time I got home, I wasn't hooked anymore, so it was pretty easy not to start again.
Interviewer: So, do you mean you've never been tempted to start smoking again?

Pat: No! In fact, I dream about it every once in a while and it's more like a nightmare.

Interviewer: Ah.

Pat: I wake up thinking, "Oh, no! I didn't start again, did I?"

Interviewer: Uh, so, Pat, uh, what advice would you give to someone who's trying to quit?

Pat: Have a heart attack. Mmm, seriously, uh, I wouldn't. I really wouldn't.

Interviewer: You wouldn't give advice?

Pat: No. So many people gave *me* advice. I gave *myself* so much advice, and to me it was meaningless. Uh, you have to decide for some reason or another that you really wanna quit, and then you will.

Narrator: Now complete the steps in your book.

Narrator: **Chapter 2, Preventing Illness**
Page 19
Restating what you have heard, Step 2

Interviewer: I'm talking with Donna, a former smoker. When did you start smoking cigarettes, Donna?

Donna: I started when I was about sixteen or seventeen years old. It was kind of a cool thing to do. A lot of my friends would get together after school and sit around and talk and smoke and eat candy–

Interviewer: Did your parents know about it?

Donna: Oh, no! God, they would've been so mad if they'd known.

Interviewer: How much did you, uh, smoke? How many–

Donna: Um, at first, just five or six cigarettes a day, but then soon after that I went up to about a pack a day.

Interviewer: Hmm.

Donna: And, um, I continued to smoke for another, y'know, *thirteen* years. In high school I, um, traveled. I lived in South America as an exchange student, and, uh, it was very common for people to smoke there.

Interviewer: Uh-huh. More so than in the United States?

Donna: Yeah. There were fewer controls. Back then people would smoke inside movie theaters, in classes. And, then later I was teaching in Mexico, and I would smoke while I was *teaching*.

Interviewer: Interesting.

Donna: Yeah, and *students* would smoke, y'know, we'd pass cigarettes around.

Interviewer: Huh.

Donna: And people smoked in *supermarkets*, in *taxicabs*, in public *buses*.

Interviewer: Um.

Donna: And then when I came back to the States, y'know, um, and I was in graduate school, we always hung out in coffee shops and drank espresso and smoked Gauloises and that was cool.

Interviewer: So, at what point did you think about quitting?

Donna: Uh, maybe two or three years after I started, I get, I started getting *sick* a lot–

Interviewer: Uh-huh.

Donna: Like, uh, I had chronic bronchitis–

Interviewer: Uh-huh.

Donna: And, um, I started trying to quit but I just couldn't.

Interviewer: Now, when you tried to quit, did you try any particular method? Or–

Donna: Initially, I just, I just went cold turkey: I just decided not to buy any more. And *that* didn't work, so then I tried the *candy* method.

Interviewer: What's the candy method?

Donna: Oh, that means you eat candy every time you want a cigarette, and *that* didn't work.

Interviewer: Did you gain weight?

Donna: Uh, I never went *long* enough! I always started smoking again within two days, maybe, and it was really painful when I stopped smoking. I couldn't sleep at night. Later, when I was pregnant, I cut back so I was hardly smoking at all, but that was really, *really* painful. I remember the first thing I did in the hospital after my son was born was go out in the hall and have a cigarette.

Narrator: Now complete the steps in your book.

Narrator: Chapter 2, Preventing Illness
Page 20
Restating what you have heard,
Step 2

Interviewer: So, Donna, how did you finally quit?

Donna: Well, I had a friend who had had a three-pack-a-day habit. And he told me about this woman who, um, *hypnotized* him, and he quit, and there was no pain at all! And so I just decided to give it a try. And it really worked!

Interviewer: Great!

Donna: Yeah, it worked for me. I had four treatments, and by the end of the fourth treatment, I had completely lost the urge to smoke.

Interviewer: Why do you think this method finally worked for you after you'd tried so many times to quit?

Donna: I think, y'know, I had just, all the other times that I'd tried to quit there had been *a part* of me that wanted to keep smoking, y'know? And I just had to reach the point where I was just ready.

Interviewer: Um-huh. Now, your son. How old is he now?

Donna: He's twelve.

Interviewer: How does *he* feel about cigarettes?

Donna: He *hated* it when I smoked – he hated the *smell*, he was afraid for my *health*. He used to put messages in my cigarette pack in my pocket saying, "Quit smoking, Mom," so that when I'd smoke I'd find them.

Interviewer: Yeah?

Donna: So he was really happy when I stopped smoking.

Interviewer: And how do you feel physically? How did you feel after you quit smoking?

Donna: The big thing I noticed – and I have a friend who quit at the same time and she noticed it too – is I just had so much more energy.

Interviewer: Huh.

Donna: And the second thing I noticed was *smells*. My sense of smell came back and I really liked being able to smell things again.

Interviewer: Did food taste better?

Donna: Oh, food tasted much better! Yeah.

Interviewer: Anything else you wanna add?

Donna: Um, the *money*!

Interviewer: Ah!

Donna: Uh, cigarettes are really expensive. When I quit, I calculated exactly how much it would cost to smoke for a year – at that time I was spending $1.50 a pack – and when I quit, I put the money in a savings account. And at the end of one year, I went out and bought myself and my son mountain bikes to celebrate our anniversary.

Interviewer: That's great.

Donna: And I've just kept doing that, and every year I use the money for something healthy to make our lives more fun.

Narrator: Now complete the steps in your book.

Narrator: Chapter 2, Preventing Illness
Page 26
Note taking: Using symbols and abbreviations, Step 3, Page 27

Narrator: One.

Lecturer: By *cardiovascular disease* I mean heart attacks, strokes, and peripheral vascular disease.

Narrator: Two.

Lecturer: *Males* appear to be at much higher risk for cardiovascular disease than females.

Narrator: Three.

Lecturer: *Obesity* technically means at least twenty percent above ideal weight. Clearly this puts a person at risk for diabetes and high blood pressure.

Narrator: Four.

Lecturer: Uh, people who've had heart attacks younger in their lives typically are what's called *Type A* personalities. You may have heard the term before. People who are, um, perfectionist, easily angry, competitive – people who work very hard and play very hard – um, these people, it's thought, tend to be under more stress and therefore under more of a risk for cardio-vascular disease.

Narrator: Now complete the steps in your book.

Narrator: Chapter 2, Preventing Illness
Page 28
Outlining practice, Step 2, Page 29

Lecturer: Today I'm going to be speaking on risk factors for cardiovascular disease. By *cardiovascular disease*, I mean heart attacks, strokes, and peripheral vascular disease, which is also known as clots to the legs. When the arteries become diseased, there's a, a loss of elasticity so that the arteries are not as flexible as they used to be. There can also be, uh, partial or complete blocking of the arteries. When a person has a heart attack, what happens is there's partial or complete blocking of the arteries which feed the *heart* muscle. In a stroke, we are talking about the blocking of one or *more* of the arteries which feed the *brain*. In peripheral vascular disease, again also known as clots to the legs, um, there's a blocking of one or more of the arteries to usually *one* of the legs.

Now there *are* risk factors which do give us an idea of who might develop one of these problems or these diseases. Uh, some of the risk factors are *alterable*. That is, the, that the person at risk can actually *do* something about them. And then there are some risk factors which are *unalterable*. I'm going to run through the *unalterable* ones first and then the alterable ones second.

OK, um, the *unalterable* risk factors are number one: *gender*. *Males* appear to be at a much higher risk for cardiovascular disease than females, at least up until about fifty years of age. Um, the simplest explanation is that estrogen, a hormone which is made in women's bodies up until menopause, appears to protect women from cardiovascular disease.

Second, *age*. As a person ages, uh, their risk of getting cardiovascular disease increases. There's not much we can do about aging, but that *is* a factor – that the older a person is, the more, the higher their risk for cardiovascular disease.

Third, *diabetes*. People with diabetes have a higher rate of cardiovascular disease. It's not known why, but unfortunately the statistics bear this out.

And then, *family history*. Uh, we all have, and *need* to have certain amounts of fats and fatty acids that our bodies use metabolically, and as long as our cholesterol and some of these other fat-containing chemicals in the blood are kept in a good, low-balanced way, they create no risk to a person. However, if they get to be in higher levels than is healthy, they *can* create a higher risk for cardiovascular disease. And this is to some extent hereditary. In fact, when you hear about youngish men, let's say men in their thirties who have heart attacks or strokes, usually it's because of family history. I mean, even if they have *other* risk factors, um, having a heart attack in one's thirties is, is very rare, and the cause is usually hereditary. So, those are the *unalterable* risk factors for cardiovascular disease.

Narrator: Now complete the steps in your book.

Narrator: Chapter 2, Preventing Illness
Page 30
Outlining practice, Step 2

Lecturer: Um, the *alterable* risk factors for cardiovascular disease include, first of all, *high blood pressure*. High blood pressure, again, does tend to run in families, but, um, there are some very, very good medications that people can take that have very few side effects in order to control high blood pressure. High blood pressure often occurs in people who are obese, uh, very overweight. But then there are many otherwise healthy people who simply have high blood pressure. And the important thing is to get these people on an appropriate medication, keep their blood pressure within normal range, and that will decrease their risk of cardiovascular disease.

Next, *obesity*. Um, some very high percentage of Americans are considered obese. *Obesity* technically means at least twenty percent *above* ideal weight. Clearly this puts a person at risk for diabetes and high blood pressure, and so it's very important to get rid of that excess weight. However, if I knew how to cure obesity, I would be an extremely wealthy woman. It's a very, very complex, uh, disease process. Usually, obese people have trouble metabolizing fats, and so generally, uh, a low-fat diet is recommended for people who are obese.

Next, uh, cigarette smoking is *clearly* a risk factor for cardiovascular disease. People who smoke cigarettes have more heart attacks and strokes *and* peripheral vascular disease, you know, blood clots in the legs. Clearly they have a higher incidence of these diseases earlier in life, than nonsmokers. Uh, the tars, the nicotines that are breathed into the bloodstream, not only raise blood pressure, but they probably also affect the way fats are metabolized as well.

And then, *stress*. If somebody does have an extremely stressful lifestyle, um, it's clearly been linked with cardiovascular disease. People who've had heart attacks younger in their lives typically are what's called *Type A* personalities. (You may have heard that term before.) People who are, um, perfectionist, easily angered, competitive people who, who work very hard and play very hard. Um, these people, it's thought, tend to be under more stress and, therefore, under more of a risk for cardiovascular disease.

Research on the Type A has been going on for over twenty years now, and *now* it's thought that there're only certain *parts* of the Type A personality that seem to increase the risk of heart disease, and those are the anger and hostility. Type A people who react with anger, people who are hostile, seem to be more at risk for heart disease, and it's important to get them to, to deal with their anger in a healthier way.

And then lastly, sedentary lifestyle has just been added as one of the alterable risk factors for cardiovascular disease. People who do not exercise, *even if* they have low blood pressure, are *not* obese, do *not* have diabetes, are *female*, *don't* smoke cigarettes, are *young*, um, keep their *stress* down and eat low-fat *diet*, people who, even if all those factors are in their favor, if a person does not exercise, they increase their chances of cardiovascular disease. So, there we go – another good reason to exercise.

Narrator: Now complete the steps in your book. This is the end of Chapter 2. This program continues on the next cassette.

3

Narrator: Cassette 2.
Chapter 3, Adolescence
Page 33
Recording numbers, Step 1

Woman: We all know from experience that children grow up at different rates, both physically and emotionally. Physically, gender accounts for the most significant difference in growth rates. In general, men end up taller than women, but that's not how it begins. Girls usually enter adolescence earlier. They start to get taller, and their bodies begin to mature sexually before boys' do.

We're going to make a graph showing typical growth patterns for adolescent boys and girls. You'll draw one line for James, a boy, and a second for Sarah, a girl. Now to make this graph, you'll need two different colored pens or pencils, or one pen and one pencil. Before we begin, complete the key next to the graph to show which pen or pencil will be for

James's growth and which for Sarah's growth.

Are you ready? Look at the graph. As you listen, make points on your graph. Later, after you finish, you can connect the points with a line.

We'll begin with James. When James was ten years old, he was four feet ten inches. He grew slowly until the age of fourteen, when he reached five feet one inch. Then he began to grow taller very quickly. By age sixteen, he was five feet eight inches tall. By eighteen, he was five feet eleven. He continued to grow taller and, by age twenty-one, James was six feet tall. He reached his full adult height, six feet one inch, at the age of twenty-two. Now take a moment to connect the points on your graph. Now you have a record of James's adolescent growth.

OK, now let's record Sarah's growth. Sarah was four feet nine inches at age ten. Then she began to grow taller at a rapid rate. By age twelve, she was five feet four inches. Her growth continued, and she reached five feet eight inches by the age of fifteen. She continued to grow, but more slowly. By age eighteen, she had reached her adult height of five feet nine inches. Now connect the points which represent Sarah's height at different ages.

Narrator: Now complete the steps in your book.

Narrator: Chapter 3, Adolescence
Page 35
Listening for specific information:
Script writing, Step 2

Interviewer: I'm talking to Eric and Jora. Jora, how old are you?

Jora: Thirteen.

Interviewer: OK, thirteen. So, that means you're in *what* grade?

Jora: Eighth.

Interviewer: OK. So, eighth grade. I'd like to ask you about your father. Can you, uh, think of a time when you wanted

to do something and he said, "Absolutely not"?

Jora: Well, yeah, just last night my girlfriend and I wanted to go to a concert downtown that was at ten thirty, and he had to be somewhere early this morning, so he didn't want to pick us up. So, I said "Well, you can take us over there"–

Interviewer: Mmm.

Jora: "And we can take a cab home." And he didn't like that, so–

Interviewer: Oh yeah.

Jora: Which I completely understand, but, you know, last night I wanted to see it from a different perspective.

Eric: See, I think two years from now I'd feel OK about it.

Interviewer: But anyway, now, you say you're willing to see his point of view about last night?

Jora: Definitely.

Interviewer: Yeah. Are there some times when you *can't* see his point of view?

Jora: Yeah, there's definitely times I can't see his point of view, but I think last night he was right.

Interviewer: Hmm. Let me ask you, Eric, how much freedom do you give Jora?

Eric: Well, I like to give Jora as much freedom as I think she's shown me she's capable of handling.

Interviewer: As much as you think she can handle. So, how does she *show* you that she can handle more freedom?

Eric: Um, for example, if, if I ask her to do something over a certain course of time, it gets done. Or by showing that she can be home at a certain time. Or if there are cases where there's a dangerous situation, that she's acted responsibly–

Interviewer: Mm-hmm.

Eric: Y'know, even if the minimum thing is just to telephone me and let me know.

Narrator: Now complete the steps in your book.

Narrator: Chapter 3, Adolescence
Page 36
Listening for main ideas, Step 2,
Page 37

Interviewer: Jora, what about things like what you
wear and make-up? Does he, does he
put his foot down on things like
that or–

Jora: Oh, it's, it's very hard to go shopping
with him sometimes–

Interviewer: Mmm.

Jora: He doesn't approve of all the clothes I
wear, of course, and he wants certain
sizes, and, and we've gotten in a few
really not pleasant fights over clothes
and, um–

Eric: On the other hand, don't you feel like
in general you're wearing the kind of
clothes that you'd like to wear?

Jora: Uh?

Eric: Well, I mean, it's not like when *I* grew
up and my parents just said, "You're
not gonna wear bellbottoms, period,"
and I didn't get them. I remember my
parents really being worried that I
was gonna turn into . . . They thought
I was gonna somehow come under
the influence–

Jora: They wanted you to be one of–

Eric: Well, they didn't want me–

Jora: To be a square?

Eric: To be a hippie.

Interviewer: Yeah?

Eric: And they didn't want me to be
involved with drugs.

Interviewer: Yeah.

Eric: And I'd say I, I certainly share *that*
concern: I don't want Jora to be part
of, a, a drug culture–

Interviewer: Yeah.

Eric: Cuz I think it is part–

Jora: Or wearing gang clothes or
something.

Eric: Yeah. And, and mostly, I guess, well,
what I'd *really* like is Jora to dress
like her*self*.

Interviewer: How does Jora feel about that?

Jora: That's fine. I mean, I don't really
wanna dress like a gang person,
anyway.

Interviewer: So, and, uh, what about make-up? Do
you wear make-up? You're not
wearing any now, are you?

Jora: No, I'm not wearing any now, but I do
wear it. I wear it to school, and my
dad has really loosened up *a lot* on
make-up.

Interviewer: Hmm.

Jora: He, uh, well he realizes that just
because he says no, I'm not gonna
not wear it.

Eric: Yeah, last year she was putting it on
at school and not telling us. I think
it's better to be open about things and
discuss them, so, as Jora says, I've
loosened up on make-up cuz I, I
mean, I'd, I'd rather she not do things
behind our backs.

Interviewer: Mmm.

Eric: I mean, *I* think she *looks* nicer
without it so–

Interviewer: Do most of your friends wear
make-up?

Jora: Yeah, some people don't, but most of
them do.

Narrator: Now complete the steps in your book.

Narrator: Chapter 3, Adolescence
Page 37
Summarizing what you have heard,
Step 2

Interviewer: So, you say Eric's what you'd consider
pretty strict but pretty fair? So, for
example, when he tells you to do
something–

Jora: Well, he's strict and I get angry when
he doesn't want me to do stuff. But
afterwards I can almost always see
why he said it, y'know?

Interviewer: Yeah.

Jora: And there's only a couple of incidents
where, well, that were totally, y'know,
that I didn't understand *at all*.

Interviewer: Hmm. Not a bad record.

Eric: No. Uh, cuz I'm sure *I've* made some
mistakes.

Interviewer: Is, how would you compare your
mom? Is she *less* strict than your dad?

Jora: Mm-hmm. Well, she's less strict, but
it's, it's like I can't win, y'know? The
stuff that my dad's not strict about my
mom's strict about, and the stuff that
my mom's not strict about, my dad is.
And, well, like my dad doesn't let me

see PG-13 or R movies, but my mom does. She, well, she rents R-rated movies, and lets me watch them and all, but my dad won't even let me see PG-13.

Eric: Well, uh, that's not really true. It depends on what it is. My rule with PG-13 is either I've had to have seen it *first* or, you know, talked to someone who I trust who's seen it.

Interviewer: So, your mom's looser about movies. Uh, what's she stricter about?

Jora: Chores, junk food, buying me specific things–

Interviewer: When you say buying you things do you mean–

Jora: Like when we go to the store.

Interviewer: She doesn't want to pay for them?

Jora: She doesn't want to pay for things. She wants me to buy my own friends' presents, you know, stuff like that.

Interviewer: So, do you get an allowance?

Jora: Yeah, I do.

Interviewer: So, Jora, what do you think about your dad? Do you think he's a pretty good dad? I mean, how does he compare with your friends' fathers?

Jora: Um, my dad *is* very *strict*, but he's, he's, he's pretty good. He, he's very nice and he lets me do just enough so I don't get too angry.

Narrator: Now complete the steps in your book.

Narrator: **Chapter 3, Adolescence**
Page 41
Note taking: Using space to show organizational structure, Step 2, Page 42

Lecturer: Now, the other common problem of adolescence that I want to speak about has to do with school performance – and that could be failing classes, acting out in class, or simply not going. Now, there are a lot of reasons for these different problems. Sometimes there are younger siblings at home who take up a lot of the parents' energy, and even though this *is* a time for teenagers to become more independent, they still need to know that they can rely on

their parents to help them through the difficulties of adolescence. So, whenever an adolescent comes into treatment with this sort of problem, we try to involve the parents immediately, and often the teenager will respond very well to having the parents become more involved in not just helping with homework, but in taking an interest in the teenager's life. So, ah, the teenager is really letting the parents know that more attention or more structure is needed. Now, what I mean by *structure* is that the parents have a clear set of rules about what behavior is expected, *and* they follow through with discipline if the child fails to meet those expectations.

Narrator: Now complete the steps in your book.

Narrator: **Chapter 3, Adolescence**
Page 43
Note-taking practice, Step 2

Lecturer: I'm going to talk about a couple of common problems of adolescents – teenagers – whom I see in mental health treatment – namely, drug and alcohol abuse, and problems at school – including acting out, poor academic performance, and truancy. Now, I'm going to talk about some of the reasons for each of these problems, and then about what we might do in treatment with these kids to see what started the problems and how we can solve them.

So, first of all, one of the problems that we see fairly frequently is teenagers who are addicted to alcohol, or some other kind of drugs. Now, why do adolescents fall into drug and alcohol abuse? Uh, in my practice, most teenagers with *severe* alcohol and drug addictions, not just recreational use, but *severe* long-term addictions, are children who have either been physically or sexually abused, or both. And these children have such intensely negative feelings about their abuse or about *themselves because* of the abuse, that the only real way they feel they can escape from or *blunt* their feelings is with drugs or alcohol.

Um, the course of treatment for these children is long and difficult, and, uh, a hospital stay is usually necessary for them to detoxify, and during that time and also *afterwards*, an intensive series of classes or, or group work is needed to help the adolescent develop the coping skills to resist the urge to go back to drugs or alcohol. These groups usually consist of people who are also in treatment or recovery programs, as well as other adolescents who have *recovered* from substance abuse, and have been able to maintain a period of sobriety for at least a year.

Once a teenager has gotten past the thirty days or sixty days of detoxification that they need, depending on the degree of addiction, that they need in order to face therapy with a clear mind and body, ah, the teenager is now more ready to talk about their feelings and about their abuse. Uh, if it was sexual abuse, they might feel guilty that they got a lot of special attention from their abuser. They might feel very *angry* and want revenge if it was physical abuse.

Now it's *very* important in the early stages of treatment that the therapist give them permission to feel *any* feelings that they have, whether they're socially acceptable or not. A person in treatment of this kind is very unsure of himself, and so a great deal of the therapist's support consists of nonjudgmental acceptance, helping the adolescent to give names to their feelings and permitting them a long period of time to experience them. Uh, this is *critical* because drugs and alcohol basically *blunt* the mind from being able to experience anything directly. We usually find that if a teenager is able to go through several months of this nonjudgmental supportive acceptance and therapy

and remain *sober*, their chances for staying away from drug or alcohol abuse in the future are fairly good.

Narrator: Now complete the steps in your book.

Narrator: **Chapter 3, Adolescence**
Page 44
Note-taking practice, Step 2

Lecturer: Now the other common problem of adolescence that I want to speak about has to do with school performance – failing classes, acting out in class, or simply not going. Now, sometimes this will begin to happen in a class where the student trusts the teacher, so often a *teacher* will be the first person to ask if there's something wrong and to refer the student for counseling. Or the problem may not be noticed until the student gets failing grades.

Now, there are a lot of reasons for these different problems, but overall this is one of a teenager's first ways of letting someone else know that there's something wrong at home. Some-times there are younger siblings who take up a lot of the parents' energy, and even though this *is* a time for teenagers to become more independent, they still need to know that they can rely on their parents to help them through the difficulties of adolescence.

So, whenever an adolescent comes into treatment with this sort of a problem, we try to involve the parents immediately, and often the teenager will respond very well to having the parents become more involved in not just helping with homework, but in taking an interest in the teenager's life. Now, of course in *some* families the parents need to become a little *less* involved in their teenager's activities and give them a chance to prove themselves on their own. But there are other times when the teenager is really letting the parents know that *more* attention or more structure is needed.

Now, what I mean by *structure* is that the parents have a clear set of rules about what behavior is expected, and what's *equally* important – they follow through with discipline if the child fails to meet those expectations. So, for example, if a child does not do well in school, the parents will allow the child to receive a failing grade rather than at the last minute doing the child's homework for him or her. And then they will talk about the problem with the child.

So, there are many times when a parent is doing either too much or too little for an adolescent child. And one of the main jobs of the therapist is to help the parent find the appropriate level of involvement.

Many of the problems that teenage clients bring to us in counseling have to do with their parents and with their home lives. And I don't think that this is any accident. Adolescents are struggling with who they are and what they can do on their own, and they still have a certain amount of need to belong to the family as a basic source of identity from which their own individual personality and independent identity can grow. If the adolescent's family life is severely disrupted or is not functioning in a way that provides this basic nurturing, this sense of identity, then the teenager is going to have difficulties developing his or her own individual sense of self.

Narrator: Now complete the steps in your book. This is the end of Chapter 3. Now please fast-forward to the end of this side and turn over the cassette to continue.

4

Narrator: Chapter 4, Adulthood
Page 47
Recording numbers, Step 1

Interviewer: Listen as I ask eight friends of mine what age they think is the best age to be. Complete the information in the chart as you listen. Bruce, how old are you?

Bruce: Twenty-eight.

Interviewer: Twenty-eight. OK, well, I wanted to ask you, whaddya think is the best age? The best period in life?

Bruce: For me, it's *these* years – late twenties, I think.

Interviewer: Yeah? Late twenties?

Bruce: Yeah.

Interviewer: Julie, may I ask how old you are?

Julie: I'm twenty-five.

Interviewer: Twenty-five? OK. And may I ask what you think the best time of life is, for you, in your opinion?

Julie: Um, I, I think the best time of life is when you're a little child.

Interviewer: Oh!

Julie: The ages four through eight or so, eight or nine.

Interviewer: Huh.

Interviewer: Ann, can you tell me how old you are?

Ann: I sure can – I'm fifty-seven. I always have to stop and think.

Interviewer: Fifty-seven. OK. Well, what I wanted to ask you about today was what do you think is the best time of life? The best age to be?

Ann: Oh, the best age to be? Oh wow, that's a great question. Definitely *not* a teenager. I think the *worst* time, if you'd asked me that, was twelve, thirteen, fourteen, fifteen. I think that's the most difficult time. The best time, I think, is probably, maybe in your thirties?

Interviewer: David, may I ask how old you are?

David: Forty-uh, almost forty-six.

Interviewer: And the, uh, the question I wanna ask you is whaddya think is the best age to be? Or, do you have an age that stands out in your mind as the best age?

David: Well, um, physically, I'd like to be, oh, uh, somewhere in my twenties, but mentally, I think I would probably have to say I'm happy to be the age that I am.

Interviewer: Otis, can I ask you how old you are?

Otis: Seventy.

Interviewer: OK. And my question is, um, what do you think is the best period of your life? What, what's the best age to be? What, what was or what is or what will be?

Otis: Oh, golly, I have to think about that. The best period, well, uh, professionally, I, uh, I think the *best* for me was like, uh, twenty-five years ago, thirty years ago.

Interviewer: Gene, what's your age?

Gene: Uh, seventy-one last week.

Interviewer: OK, and Laurie, how old are you?

Laurie: I'm sixty-eight, sixty-nine next month.

Interviewer: OK, and so, the question I want to ask is what do you think . . . what is the best age to be? How about you, Laurie?

Laurie: To be the age you are is the best age to be, so I love the age I am right now.

Interviewer: Well, were there any periods in your life that you enjoyed more than others?

Laurie: Um. *Yes*, my forties were *wonderful*.

Interviewer: And, Gene, how about you? What do you consider the best age to be, for yourself? The best period in your life?

Gene: Gee, I dunno.

Interviewer: Loleta, first I wanna ask you *how* old are you?

Loleta: I'm seventy-seven.

Interviewer: OK. Seventy-seven. And the question I wanna ask you is whaddya think is the best age to be? For you?

Loleta: Well, I look back at special times in my life and, oh, the period between graduation from college and getting married was wonderful for me.

Narrator: Now complete the steps in your book.

Narrator: Chapter 4, Adulthood
Page 48
Answering true/false questions,
Step 2, Page 49

Interviewer: OK, Bruce, um, why is the late twenties better than, say, *earlier* twenties?

Bruce: Um, I think that when you're in your, in the early twenties, you're just getting over, um, teenage adolescent years, so now I think in the late twenties you kinda know a direction but, um, the early twenties are just too . . . you just kinda remember too many things of the teenage years and you're still trying to get a plan. But in the twenties, *late* twenties, you kind of know what you wanna do and you kind of have an idea of, of how to get it. *And* you know how to settle down, too. You can see a plan for getting things and also settling down.

Interviewer: Hmm. Um, is there a time in your life that you think you would call the *most difficult* time?

Bruce: Probably the teenage years, like fourteen, fifteen–

Interviewer: Yeah?

Bruce: Sixteen.

Interviewer: The mid teens.

Bruce: Yeah, I think the mid teens were the worst.

Interviewer: So, Julie, why would you like to be a little girl again?

Julie: Um, I think, uh, I think lately because the age I'm at now, I feel is kind of a stressful age.

Interviewer: Huh.

Julie: When you're, when you're younger, you don't have as many worries and responsibilities.

Interviewer: Yeah.

Julie: You don't have all the *stresses* of life as an adult. I think at the age I'm at now, when you get out of college and you need to find a job–

Interviewer: Uh-huh.

Julie: And I'm single and I can't depend on my parents anymore–

Interviewer: Uh-huh.

Julie: And I have new responsibilities – just trying to get *used* to having new responsibilities – and also figure out what I wanna do – there's lots of decisions.

Interviewer: Uh-huh.

Julie: I don't always know what the best thing to do is. Um, those are things that I need to learn.

Interviewer: Yeah.

Julie: Yeah!

Interviewer: So, Ann, why was being in your thirties good?

Ann: Because in your thirties you pretty much know what you like and what you don't like, and you're kind of settled into life. And, at least for me, that was a really good time. Actually, now that my sons are married and, and they're independent–

Interviewer: Uh-huh.

Ann: When I come to come to think about it, I probably do more interesting things now for *myself* than I did when I was in my thirties.

Interviewer: Huh! For example–

Ann: Well, now I'm playing in an orchestra, which I would never've had time to do when, when the boys were little and, um, and I, uh, read a lot more than I did.

Interviewer: Do you and your husband go out more?

Ann: Ha! We do! We do. We go out to movies, and we go out to dinner, and we hope to be able to travel!

Narrator: Now complete the steps in your book.

Narrator: Chapter 4, Adulthood
Page 50
Summarizing what you have heard, Step 2

Interviewer: So, Otis, uh, professionally your early forties were your best time, you say?

Otis: Yeah. Well, actually, I would say maybe from, um, thirty-five to about fifty.

Interviewer: Why was that?

Otis: Um, I was much more receptive to new ideas, I lectured better, I *read* a lot more, and I was very interested in doing certain things in a different way.

Interviewer: Uh-huh.

Otis: Because when I was fifty, actually, is when I *created* about four courses that had never been taught at the university here before. I'd just come to the university, and I created all those courses and taught them regularly, and most of them *worked*.

Interviewer: That's great.

Otis: But I think in terms of feeling mature and responsible and, um, sensitive to the world around me, I think the last ten years have been the best.

Interviewer: OK.

Interviewer: So, what was so wonderful about your forties, Laurie?

Laurie: Well, cuz, well, I had, I had basically educated myself cuz I got my master's degree during my forties and that was a *very* exciting time – I *really* enjoyed that a *lot*. And, um, my children had grown up so I was beginning to feel *free* of a lot of my responsibilities and commitments, and I could focus on my own work, which is painting. And I also started studying *music*, which was really great cuz I hadn't done that before. And I met some wonderful people. It was a beginning.

Interviewer: So, Gene, you say you don't know what age is best, but is there any period in your life that you really loved more than others or–

Gene: The older, the older I get, the more I think about when I was younger but, but that's probably . . . I think the older you get, the more you think about your youth.

Interviewer: And the more–

Gene: At least when you get past a certain age.

Interviewer: Yeah, and the more you value it? The more you miss it?

Gene: Yeah. You know, when you're younger, you can't wait to grow up. And when you're old, you think, "What an idiot I was, and I should've understood that there were, that there were things that weren't quite so bad then," y'know. But you don't know when you're younger. For instance, you get up and you feel, "Well, the world is terrific," y'know. But when you're older and you wake up, I mean, you don't feel so well, you know. I mean, you gotta, your bones hurt and your joints hurt and you gotta kind of, um, well, it takes a mental effort to get . . . and sometimes it takes like, uh, Laurie and I always talk about how long it takes to get *going* in the morning, y'know. In the army, we used to get up and ten minutes later we were out on the parade field. And now when we get up we gotta do our exercises. Then we gotta do our *walk*. Then we gotta do our *bath*. I mean, it's like our *job* now. We don't have *time* to work anymore.

Narrator: Now complete the steps in your book.

Narrator: **Chapter 4, Adulthood**
Page 54
Note taking: Paying attention to signal words, Step 3, Page 55

Narrator: One.
Lecturer: By *developmental tasks*, uh, I mean life changes that a person must accomplish, as, uh, as he or she grows and develops.
Narrator: Two.
Lecturer: What we expect at this point is for the, um, the young adult to be supporting him- or herself completely, that includes financially, emotionally, and socially.
Narrator: Three.
Lecturer: The, the old relationship, uh, in which the child related to his parents in a hierarchical way – that is, *solely as parents* – this relationship changes.
Narrator: Four.
Lecturer: The result is that it's often very difficult for, uh, for young adults to survive without financial assistance from their parents.
Narrator: Five.
Lecturer: So, as I said, it can be difficult for young adult children to establish financial independence from their parents.
Narrator: Six.
Lecturer: Of course separation is the natural thing for adult children to do. But *even though* it's natural, this is still a crisis point in a family – when a child leaves.
Narrator: Seven.
Lecturer: So, we've talked about two of the important tasks of young adulthood.

Narrator: Now complete the steps in your book.

Narrator: **Chapter 4, Adulthood**
Page 56
Note-taking practice, Step 2

Lecturer: I'm going to speak about, uh, two of the major developmental tasks of young adulthood, and, uh, by *developmental tasks*, I mean life changes that a person must accomplish as he or she grows and develops. The young adult is in his or her early to mid-twenties, and, uh, at least in *Western* culture, this is the time for the achievement of independence from their parents. *Ideally*, what's considered optimal at this point is for the, uh, for the young adult to be capable of supporting him- or herself completely – well, that includes financially, emotionally, and socially

OK, so, uh, we could say that one of the major tasks for young adults is the development of a new and different type of relationship with parents. The old relationship, uh, in, in which the child related to his parents in a hierarchical way – that is, *solely as parents* – well, uh, this relationship changes in the young adult years, and, uh, a new kind of relationship is established, one based on mutual adulthood. This is the sort of culmination of a long process of separation that starts in early childhood, and ideally in young adulthood the child *physically* separates and goes his or her own way in the world. Uh, interestingly enough, this is a change that seems to be happening later in life, in, uh, in the, in the latter part of the twentieth century, partly because it depends on the child's ability to become *financially* independent, and in today's world, uh, there is so much competition for jobs. Uh, the cost of living continues to rise. Well, the result is that it's often very difficult for young adults to survive without financial assistance from their parents, and so, uh, sometimes that means that they simply stay at home and live with their parents, uh, well, well into their twenties.

So, as I said, it, it can be difficult for young-adult children to establish *financial* independence from their parents. And then, establishing *emotional* independence can, uh, can also be a difficult process, and not all children separate from their parents with, with equal success. Some children may never be successful at this. They may be forever in the role of child and parent forever in the role of parent.

Of course, uh, separation is the natural thing for adult children to do at this point – to, to leave their parents and start their own lives. But, even though it's natural, this is still a crisis point in a family, when a child leaves and, uh, and some families don't handle it well. Change is, uh, a frightening thing for many people, but there's no escaping it. Uh, we *all* have to learn how to change throughout our lives.

Narrator: Now complete the steps in your book.

Narrator: Chapter 4, Adulthood
Page 57
Note-taking practice, Step 2

Lecturer: And then there's a second task of young adulthood, which ties into this whole business of, uh, getting married. Erik Erikson identifies, um, uh, the period of young adulthood as the time when the young adult faces the crisis of intimacy versus isolation. Well, the theory is that in adolescence the child has developed a healthy identity, and, uh, of course in reality, for a variety of reasons, many people fail to develop this healthy identity in adolescence, uh, but again, *ideally*, then, uh, in young adulthood, this identity is ready and able to be joined with another, traditionally in marriage. This involves the ability to make a *commitment* to someone, uh, in a close intimate way. Now, uh, according to Erikson, uh, healthy

people during this period are able to compromise, to sacrifice, to, to negotiate – all of which one *must* do to make a marriage successful. This, then, as I said, is a second major development task, uh, developmental task of this period. The ability to adapt to another person in this way will, uh, will increase intimacy, or closeness and connection. Now, the *in*ability to do this will leave the individual alone and self-absorbed. So, there you have *intimacy* or *isolation*, and the challenge for the young adult is to resolve that crisis, and, as I said, uh, success depends on the young adult having developed a healthy, a *solid*, healthy identity in adolescence.

Um, it's difficult to give yourself to another person in a relationship, uh, if you do not have a self to give, if your *self* is not defined, uh, if it is not solid, and, uh, it puts great emotional stress and strain on a relationship when, uh, when two people are in the process of, of trying to deal with the developmental tasks of marriage, when they haven't yet dealt with the important developmental tasks involved in just, uh, in just being a separate person. That, ideally, *should* come first.

So, the developmental task of solving the crisis of intimacy versus isolation – uh, we traditionally associate this task with marriage. But let me say that, uh, *increasingly*, in the West, staying single has become an acceptable alternative to, uh, to being married. Uh, people who in the past might have felt pressure to marry in their early twenties, right out of college, may now have more freedom to be single for a longer period of time. Uh, with this is the freedom, for example, to take more risks, to move to a different part of the country or to a different part of the world. And there is *also*, with, what with the divorce rate as high as it is, a certain, uh, reluctance, a, a skepticism about marriage as an institution. As a result, um, many young adults are, are, are waiting to get married, uh, until their late twenties or older. And, uh, in fact the statistics show that couples who *do* wait till their late twenties to get married have a much lower divorce rate than those who marry in their early twenties.

So, we've, uh, we've talked about two of the important tasks of young adulthood: the first, *separation* from parents, which, uh, involves renegotiating one's, uh, one's relationship with parents; and the second, solving the crisis of *intimacy* versus *isolation*, uh, that is, bringing a, uh, a *solid* sense of one's self to a relationship with another person. And, uh, the degree of success with which the young adult accomplishes these tasks will determine to a great extent their future success and satisfaction in life.

Narrator: Now complete the steps in your book. This is the end of Chapter 4. The program continues on the next cassette.

5

Narrator: Cassette 3.
Chapter 5, Assessing Intelligence
Page 61
Listening to directions, Step 1

Man: You are going to hear several questions similar to those you would find on an intelligence assessment test. Just follow the directions that you hear.

Are you ready? OK. For questions one through four, write short answers in your book. You will have five seconds each to answer questions one and two.

Number one: What is the capital of Egypt?

Number two: What would you do if your neighbor's house were on fire?

You will have fifteen seconds each for questions three and four.

Number three: Without using paper or pencil, find the answer: If a train travels at a hundred fifty kilometers an hour, how far will it go in ninety minutes?

Number four: Again without paper or pencil: If a boy will be twice as old as his sister next year, and he is now four years older than she is, what are their ages now?

For questions five and six, say your answers out loud. Do not write anything.

Number five: Listen and repeat out loud the following numbers: two – four – eight – three – nine – one – six – five

Number six: Listen and repeat out loud – *backwards* – the following numbers: seven – eight – four – three – two – six

Number seven: How are a horse and a car alike? Write as many similarities as you can in twenty seconds.

Number eight: Look at the four pictures in your book. Quickly arrange them in order to tell a story. Write the numbers under the pictures.

Number nine: You have fifteen seconds: What does the word *prejudice* mean? Write your answer.

Narrator: Now complete the steps in your book.

Narrator: Chapter 5, Assessing Intelligence
Page 63
Listening for specific information, Step 2

Interviewer: Ruth, do you remember back in elementary and junior high school, how there were always the so-called *smart* kids, and then there were the kids that didn't do so well?

Ruth: Yeah, I do, I remember that. I remember, um, being one of the smarter kids, and I remember particularly in elementary school, just, they had the reading groups, you know, first, second, and third.

Interviewer: Yeah, I remember.

Ruth: And, uh, being in the first reading group and kind of not getting, you know, like what exactly were the second and third reading groups for? What, what did they do there?

Interviewer: Yeah.

Ruth: And I remember also very vividly being, um, one of those kids that other kids would come over and say, "How do you spell *people*?" – y'know.

Interviewer: Yeah.

Ruth: And, and I'd say "oh, P-E-O-P-L-E" and I'd think, "How do I know that?" And I would *think*, I remember thinking, "Oh, I think it has to do with *reading*."

Interviewer: Uh-huh.

Ruth: I somehow . . . and I just remember that.

Interviewer: Because you liked to read and maybe they didn't read as much as you did.

Ruth: Yeah! I remember trying to tell my brother. My brother *struggled* in school, and I remember – one of the things he really struggled with was spelling – and I remember trying *really hard*–

Interviewer: He's older than you, right?

Ruth: Yeah, he's two years older than I am. And I remember trying really hard to help him with his spelling and trying to share with him how I remembered how to spell words that didn't – they didn't follow a *pattern* – these words, they were–

Interviewer: Ah, irregular spellings.

Ruth: Irregular spellings. And, so, I would kind of make funny little . . . I'm trying to think of an example . . . I can't think of an example, but, just, I would, I would make little songs out of them, the words, and make them so that I would remember that there was a silent *e* at the end. Or there was a silent *h* or something like that, and that would help me, and he could not *get* that. It just, *my system* just didn't work for him, and I sort of just threw my hands up.

Interviewer: Uh-huh.

Ruth: Ahh!

Interviewer: Yeah.

Ruth: Y'know.

Narrator: Now complete the steps in your book.

Narrator: Chapter 5, Assessing Intelligence
Page 63
Listening for specific information,
Step 2, Page 64

Interviewer: So, Ruth, you feel like you did well in school basically without ever really trying or without much effort.

Ruth: Yeah, yeah, I did. School was, it was *not hard* for me. It was, I en*joyed* it. It was positive; the learning part of it was very positive for me and it wasn't until I was in junior high school, seventh grade, and I got to, uh, algebra that I was really just, I all of a sudden encountered something that I did not understand – I did *not get* it, and I didn't know how to *work* to get it. I didn't know how to–

Interviewer: You either got it or you didn't–

Ruth: You either got it or you didn't–

Interviewer: Yeah.

Ruth: Yeah. And by not getting it I just, I just remember being shocked! I can't, I don't get this! And I didn't know to turn to somebody for *help*. I, I, I just did *not* know what to *do*. And so I just kind of floundered through and, um, developed this belief that, that I just wasn't *good* at that subject, but the interesting thing was I was always fascinated by mathematics. And later in college I had several friends who were majoring in mathematics, and I had a lot of rapport with them and shared a lot of their ways of thinking, and I wondered why, why I could be good at that *verbally*, but not good at it on pencil and paper.

Interviewer: Yeah.

Ruth: But that first experience of not being able to get it was, um, I mean, I've often wondered how I could have dealt with that *differently*. And how I could really, uh, how I could have made that work.

Interviewer: Yeah.

Ruth: I think what happened when I was in junior *high* school, is that I kind of labeled myself as not good at that subject.

Interviewer: Which is probably what the kids in reading group three were doing back in elementary school.

Ruth: Yeah! Exactly, of course, and so that was kind of a, that was something I could do to make that OK.

Interviewer: So, you told yourself that there was nothing you could do about it, you just weren't good at math.

Ruth: Exactly.

Narrator: Now complete the steps in your book.

Narrator: **Chapter 5, Assessing Intelligence
Page 64
Retelling, Step 2, Page 65**

Ruth: Y'know, this reminds me of this, this story that I read somewhere recently about this man who went through school–

Interviewer: Uh-huh.

Ruth: And at some point early in his school career, I think it must have been early in high school–

Interviewer: Um-huh.

Ruth: He was basically told, um, that he was a *dunce*!

Interviewer: Oh, no.

Ruth: That he was of very low intelligence and that he really shouldn't have much, that he, he shouldn't expect too much.

Interviewer: In terms of a career.

Ruth: Yeah, in terms of a career and stuff. And so that's how he viewed himself. So he went off in life and he, uh, he got a real . . . kind of structured his *life* to *match* the label that he gave himself.

Interviewer: Which, which had been given him–

Ruth: Yeah, cuz he adopted that, the label that, that the school gave him, he took as his own.

Interviewer: He believed it.

Ruth: He believed it because it was, y'know, based on a test that they had given him.

Interviewer: Yeah, a test! Oh, it must be true! A test.

Ruth: Oh, yeah! What else is there to say? So he went out and got, y'know, a very low-paying, menial-type job and,

uh, was just going along in life, and I don't remember just exactly how this happened, but somehow, um, his IQ was tested again.

Interviewer: Um-huh.

Ruth: And the determination was made that he was not in fact of low intelligence, but he was of very *high* intelligence–

Interviewer: Amazing.

Ruth: And *in fact* he was in the genius category.

Interviewer: Amazing.

Ruth: I mean, like, his IQ was measured at about a hundred and sixty or something, and then, he again relied on the written test – he took that information and the new label, internalized it, and went out and changed his *whole* life to match that new information.

Interviewer: Huh!

Ruth: He, um, became a successful *business*man, and he made a lot of money, and he, he just, y'know, he changed *everything*–

Interviewer: Yeah?

Ruth: About his *whole* life, with this new information. It was just kind of *fascinating*, y'know.

Interviewer: Yeah!

Ruth: I mean, he was always the same person – he *always* had that same *intelligence*, but he–

Interviewer: Uh-huh!

Ruth: You know, the *test*!

Interviewer: The test. Huh!

Narrator: Now complete the steps in your book.

Narrator: **Chapter 5, Assessing Intelligence
Page 68
Note taking: Recognizing examples,
Step 2, Page 69**

Narrator: One.

Lecturer: So, Binet came up with tasks that he thought were important for success in school, such as good memory skills, reasoning skills, and, uh, verbal comprehension skills.

Narrator: Two.

Lecturer: And then he *age-graded* these tasks. He said, for example, um, with the memory tasks that a five-year-old should be able to remember a list of, say, three words, and a seven-year-old should be able to remember five words, and so on.

Narrator: Three.

Lecturer: Binet figured out what the mental age for a *normal* child would be, in other words, how many tasks the average five-year-old, six-year-old, seven-year-old, and so on, uh, could do.

Narrator: Four.

Lecturer: So, by definition, an average child has an IQ of a hundred. Now, let's take an example: Say you have a nine-and-a-half-year-old child who has a mental age of seven. Let's figure out his IQ by the formula. We divide seven by nine point five, which is about point seven four. Now we multiply by one hundred, giving us a below-average IQ of seventy-four for this child.

Narrator: Five.

Lecturer: We find that people who grow up in environments that don't value formal education are not going to do well on a traditional IQ test. Whether or not they have *intelligence*, though, is a whole different matter. For example, I know that I would have a really hard time surviving, uh, in a rough neighborhood, where you need street smarts in order to get along. I don't think anybody really cares in that sort of situation how many books I've read or what my IQ score is.

Narrator: Now complete the steps in your book.

Narrator: **Chapter 5, Assessing Intelligence**
Page 70
Outlining practice, Step 2

Lecturer: Modern intelligence testing began with Alfred Binet in 1905. At that time the French government had recently passed a law requiring all children to attend school. And suddenly, teachers had a much wider range of students to deal with. So they had to be able to *identify* the students who needed special help. Binet was hired by the government to create a test to identify students who were below average academically. So, how did Binet go about trying to, uh, devise his test? He needed to have a premise or a theory on which to base the test, and the theory which he used is that intelligence increases with age. Intelligence increases with age: that the older one got, the smarter one got. So, if we tested a number of students on a number of tasks, we'd probably find that the older students would be able to do more tasks than the younger students, ah – that they would be *smarter*, in a sense.

So, Binet came up with a huge assortment of tasks that used different skills that he thought were important for success in school, such as good memory skills, reasoning skills, and, uh, verbal comprehension skills – those were all important, all important, for success in school. And then he *age-graded* these tasks. He said, for example, with the memory tasks that a five-year-old should be able to remember a list of, say, three words, and a seven-year-old should be able to remember five words, and so on. And depending on how many of these tasks a child could do – and they get progressively more difficult – when a child came to a point where they could no longer do any more tasks, at that point we say we've reached the child's *mental age*. And this is a big concept in, in Binet's theory, this idea of a mental age *score* depending on how many tasks a child could do.

So, Binet figured out what the mental age for a *normal* child would be, in other words, how many tasks the average five-year-old, six-year-old, seven-year-old, and so on, could do. And if a seven-year-old could do all of the tasks that an average *nine*-year-old could do, we would say that that seven-year-old was very bright. If a five-year-old could only do the tasks that a three-year-old could do, we would say that that five-year-old was dull and would have some learning problems. So, this is how Binet used his test – to identify the students who were slow learners. And that, that's important to keep in *mind*: that, uh, the original purpose of his test was *only* to identify students who might have trouble in school.

Well, after Binet's death in 1911, Lewis Terman, who, uh, was then a professor at Stanford, he revised and extended Binet's test for use with teenagers and adults, and this *revised* test came to be known as the Stanford-Binet, which is still in use today. The Stanford-Binet, um, came up with the idea of a *ratio* measure of intelligence that we now call an *IQ* or an *intelligence quotient*. And the way that one *determines* an IQ is by dividing the child's mental age – which as you remember depends on how many tasks they can do – dividing that by the *chronological* age – in years and months – and multiplying that by a hundred. So, by this formula, by definition, an average child has an IQ of a hundred.

Now, let's take an example: Say you have a nine-and-a-half-year-old child who has a mental age of seven. Let's figure out his IQ by the formula. We divide seven by nine point five, which is about point seven four. Now, we multiply by one hundred, giving us a below-average IQ of seventy-four for this child. Again, the thing to remember about Binet's test is that Binet designed it *only* to identify which children are going to have learning problems in school, and that, that seems to have gotten lost in our current usage of IQ tests. We now use them for, um, job placement, and, um, for other purposes for which the test was *not* created. This is *not* what Binet had in mind.

Narrator: Now complete the steps in your book.

Narrator: Chapter 5, Assessing Intelligence
Page 71
Outlining practice, Step 2

Lecturer: Current approaches to IQ testing – um, another thing to know about the Binet is that it's very long, it's very complicated, it takes a *long* time to administer. And, um, in 1939 the psychologist David Wechsler created one of the most widely used intelligence tests today – the Wechsler Scales. Today there are three separate Wechsler tests for different age groups, and, uh, the Wechsler scales are different from the Binet scales in that they're easier to administer, and also they test not only verbal skills but also performance abilities, such as putting together puzzles and some other visual-spatial skills.

Some problems with, uh, IQ testing we need to keep in mind: First, what does, what does intelligence mean? Does it mean that you have a high IQ score? Um, if *so*, then what does that IQ score predict? Does it predict *life* success? Um, or *job* success? And the answer is *no*. IQ is related to *school* success, but it's *not* related to *job* success. It's not related to life success in, uh, any significant way.

So, one of the problems with using intelligence *tests*, uh, to rank people is that we really don't know exactly what it is that we're measuring. We really, we know we're measuring *something*, but, uh, we, we really don't know if that thing is intelligence. The other issue that we need to, uh, keep in mind is that intelligence tests as we know them have a very strong cultural bias in favor of educated middle- or upper-class individuals. Um, we, we find that people who grow up in environments that don't value formal education are not going to do well on a traditional IQ test. Whether or not they have *intelligence*, though, is a whole different matter. For example, I know that I would have a really hard time surviving in, uh, in a rough neighborhood, where you need street smarts in order to get along. I don't think anybody really cares in that sort of situation how many books I've read or what my IQ score is. A, a child who's grown up in that area and who's learned to survive and thrive is, uh, much more intelligent than I am in that situation, but that certainly won't show up on an IQ test. So, we have to, uh, keep in mind that the traditional IQ tests miss a lot of what it takes to be successful in different environments – uh, in, in fact, in *any* environment except for school.

Those were the three major topics that I wanted to cover today: the history of intelligence testing beginning with Binet's work, the current approaches, and some problems with intelligence assessment.

Narrator: Now complete the steps in your book. This is the end of Chapter 5. Now please fast-forward to the end of this side and turn over the cassette to continue.

6

Narrator: Chapter 6, Accounting for Variations in Intelligence
Page 73
Recording numbers, Step 2

Woman: The Scholastic Assessment Test, or the SAT, is given every year to high school seniors. Scores range from a low of 200 to a high of 800. Now, in this exercise, you will hear verbal and *math* scores for males and females for selected years between 1972 and 1996. You'll need two different colored pens, or a pen and a pencil. Use one to mark the female scores and the other to mark the male scores. As you hear each score, make a dot on the graph. Later, you can connect the dots to make lines. Before we start, use your pens or pen and pencil to complete the key below the graphs.

Are you ready? We'll do the male verbal scores first.

In 1972, the average male score on the *verbal* section of the SAT was 531. By 1976, it had dropped to 513, and in 1980, to 507. Scores then *climbed* a bit, up to 510 in 1984, and 515 in 1986. They dropped again to 504 in 1992, and in 1996, the average male score on the verbal section was 507.

Now let's turn to the average *math* scores for males.

In 1972, the average male score on the math section of the SAT was 527. It was down *seven* points to 520 in 1976, and down to 515 in 1980. In 1984, the average male math score was up a little to 519. It was 522 in 1988, then dropped one point in 1992 to 521. Finally, in 1996, the average math score for males was up to 527.

Now change to your other pen or pencil. Let's look at how *females* did on the SAT between 1972 and 1996. First, the verbal section.

In 1972, the average female score was 529. It fell to 508 in 1976, then again to 499 four years later in 1980. It was down one point in 1984 to 498, then rose to a high of 504 in 1986. Then in 1992 it was down to 496, and up again sharply in 1996 to 503.

Now math scores for females from 1972 to 1996.

The 1972 score was 489. It then began to fall – to 474 in 1976 – and it fell one more point, to 473, in 1980. It climbed *slightly* to 478 in 1984, and was up to 483 in 1988. In 1992, the average female math score was up one point to 484, and then began to climb steadily to 492 in 1996.

Narrator: Now complete the steps in your book.

Narrator: Chapter 6, Accounting for Variations in Intelligence
Page 75
Listening for specific information, Step 2

Interviewer: Dennis, how many years have you been working in education?

Dennis: Well! It's been twenty-three years now.

Interviewer: Uh-huh!

Dennis: First as a classroom teacher, in high school, middle school, and, but mostly at the elementary level, in third and fourth grade. And then I spent five years as an elementary school principal, and then this year I'm working as a director of education programs.

Interviewer: OK! Well, what I wanted to ask you about first is what differences have you seen, um, between the way *girls* perform, and the ways *boys* perform at various ages?

Dennis: Yeah, well, there's the difference that's really become a *cliché*, and *that* is that girls' performance in math and science courses tends to drop off in the late middle school years.

Interviewer: Uh-huh.

Dennis: And on the other end, in primary grades, girls, because of generally earlier acquisition of language and fine motor skills and, I dunno, maybe generally better behavior, do do *better*. So, in the primary grades the boys are usually behind the girls, and generally the really strong popular leaders in the classroom are girls.

Interviewer: Uh-huh.

Dennis: And then around fourth and fifth grade, boys, y'know, start asserting themselves but in different ways from girls.

Interviewer: How so?

Dennis: Well, *I* think one of the *big* differences in how girls and boys perform is how, y'know, they get *attention*. I think boys are a lot more comfortable doing things that are unexpected, y'know, being slightly inappropriate but not to the point of really getting in trouble. Whereas I think, in girls – and again I'm talking about what *third*- and *fourth*-graders do to get attention in class – with girls it's, it's still more things like doing a really good job on your homework and always raising your hand for questions–

Interviewer: Yeah!

Dennis: That sort of thing. Yeah. Boys seem to be a little more comfortable doing things that are not expected, asserting themselves against the teacher. And this behavior seems to become more acceptable as we get into the higher grades.

Interviewer: Uh-huh.

Dennis: Um, and then, as for *girls*, y'know, in *middle* school years, um, I think, y'know, again, the cliché is is that they feel the need to kinda *dumb down* a little bit because the issue of being attractive to boys, y'know. Getting *attention* from boys is so important, so girls don't wanna do anything that's gonna interfere with that.

Interviewer: Uh-huh. So, is it really *documented* that girls, um, start to do worse at that age in math and science?

Dennis: Yeah, it is. It's been written about a lot in the educational journals, and I guess my experience supports the research that I've read.

Interviewer: Yeah.

Dennis: Yeah, that's the pattern that we see, especially on math tests, starting in late middle school, say around age fourteen.

Narrator: Now complete the steps in your book.

Narrator: Chapter 6, Accounting for Variations in Intelligence
Page 75
Listening for specific information, Step 2, Page 76

Interviewer: Dennis, are there any other explanations for why girls don't do well in math classes?

Dennis: Well, I think one important issue which affects both boys *and* girls is how teachers traditionally ask questions – uh, how a question is assigned and how soon the answer is expected. Uh, the cognitive research people have a lot of data about this, and basically what they say is, first of all, just in a traditional teacher question/answer style, questions tend to be assigned very quickly. Y'know, "Who's the fifteenth president of the United States? Miriam!" Y'know, just assign the question right away, and basically there's no time for thinking.

So what happens is it causes a level of tension in the classroom, which causes everybody to temporarily move to another part of their brain, and the person being asked the *question* generally can't *think of* the *answer*.

Interviewer: Yeah.

Dennis: I think a lot of people have had that experience where they're trying to think of something and they just can't find it, and then once they relax, the information comes up?

Interviewer: Yeah.

Dennis: And that's because you're moving back to another part of your brain once the stress decreases.

Anyway, this rapid-fire question/answer pattern is quite common in high school math classes, and there's been some very interesting research done on the amount of *time* given by, y'know, *traditional* math teachers. The amount of time given a *boy* to respond is longer than the amount of time given a girl, and not because the teacher has decided consciously, "Well, I'm gonna *do* this," but *generally* it has to do with the teacher's expectation, and the expectation is, "Well, the *boy* has a better chance of, of getting this, so we'll wait a little longer." But if it's a girl student, or, or someone you don't anticipate is going to be very *successful* with it, then you don't wait as long because you want to keep that fast question/answer pattern moving. So, it's part of that rapid-fire questioning strategy which really doesn't work very well for human brains anyway.

Interviewer: Yeah!

Dennis: And sometimes puts girls at a disadvantage because of the *actual* amount of time they're given.

Narrator: Now complete the steps in your book.

Narrator: Chapter 6, Accounting for Variations in Intelligence
Page 76
Listening for specific information, Step 2

Interviewer: Dennis, let me ask you a different question, and that is do you think that a child's economic and maybe social background makes a difference in school performance?

Dennis: Yeah, y'know, there *is* a pattern. The elementary school where I had most of my teaching experience and where I eventually became principal, uh, was an interesting one because it sat between two very different parts parts of, of this *community*. Uh, one part is a very wealthy neighborhood built around a world-class golf course. And then the *other* part of the community is low-income housing, including a complex for families, um, where the mother has just been released from the local women's *prison*. So, y'know, I really saw a wide economic and social range, and, and I've seen low-income families that just do a great job of getting their kids to school and supporting them in their education. But, y'know, I think the predictable cliché there is true – that those kids who are *supported*, *do* better. Kids whose parents value education do better. And, y'know, *another* big economic issue is *technology* – access to computers. The kids who have multimedia computers at home in their bedrooms – they just do better!

Interviewer: Yeah.

Dennis: With computers there's a realization starting to develop that it's, it's not just technological skills, but there are also some *thinking* skills that improve with, with being able to organize your information that way, y'know.

Interviewer: Yeah!

Dennis: Some of these kids can really turn out some outstanding work and, and the *content* has improved too, not just the presentation. So, I think there, there are some real differences based on economic background, and they just compound with each generation. That's been my experience. But, y'know, there's no guarantee because you have all this support at home that you're gonna do well, too. I mean, I've seen some kids, pretty wealthy kids, just totally *blow* it, and, uh, not be productive and, and not even stay in *school*. Or there are the cases where you've got, y'know, one kid who does great, and then the other sibling in the same environment is just *totally*, totally out of control!

Interviewer: Does that happen?

Dennis: Well, it's kind of like a movie cliché again, but yeah, it does sometimes happen.

Interviewer: Speaking of families, do siblings *usually* perform at about the same level in school?

Dennis: Yeah, in *families*, usually, there tends to be a pattern, I think. I mean, like kids who tend to be kinesthetically intelligent – I've noticed that seems to run in families.

Interviewer: Can you explain what you mean by *kinesthetic intelligence*?

Dennis: Well, yeah, this is from Howard Gardner's theory of multiple intelligences. These are kids, y'know, for whom muscle memory and coordination, uh, y'know, they look at a basketball play and, and perceive the information on a whole different level from a lot of other kids who don't necessarily have kinesthetic intelligence, and so suddenly they are able to go out there and replicate these movements and things. I mean, I think basketball's a great one because of what it takes to, to aggressively drive to the basket. Y'know, for some kids it's just a lot easier task than it is for others. You definitely see some kids who really excel at that.

Narrator: Now complete the steps in your book.

Narrator: **Chapter 6, Accounting for Variations in Intelligence**
Page 81
Note taking: Recording numbers, Step 2

Narrator: One.

Lecturer: Um, first, on the nature side, uh, William Tryon in the 1940s – he was working with rats.

Narrator: Two.

Lecturer: We know that the correlation of IQ scores for identical twins that are raised together in the same environment is about point eight five, which is *very*, very significant. And even identical twins who are raised *apart*, in *different* environments, *still* have an IQ correlation of point seven two, which again *is* significant. Uh, however, if heredity were the *only* factor, then the correlation between identical twins, whether they were raised together *or apart*, should be at one.

Narrator: Three.

Lecturer: Fraternal twins – their correlation is point six. Siblings who are raised together – the correlation is about point four five.

Narrator: Four.

Lecturer: We've also found in studies with *kids*, when we take disadvantaged, inner-city kids and put them in middle-class, suburban homes where education is valued, after a period of time, we tend to see a *jump* in IQ of about fifteen points, uh, over the IQs of similar kids that are raised in a more impoverished, inner-city environment.

Narrator: Now complete the steps in your book.

Narrator: Chapter 6, Accounting for Variations in Intelligence
Page 82
Listening for specific information, Step 2

Lecturer: What is it that determines intelligence? One of the *big* debates among research is is intelligence something that is inherited? Is it something that's part of a person's biological make-up? Or is intelligence the result of environmental influences? This is the old nature-nurture debate, as it relates to intelligence. Uh, we have both animal and human evidence on *both* sides of the issue, and, uh, let me really start by saying that there *is* no *answer* to the nature-nurture question, or rather the answer is that *both* nature *and* nurture play a role in the development of intelligence, and it's really difficult to determine the relative influence of each.

But as I said, we have evidence on, from *both* animal and human studies, on *both* sides of the issue. Um, first, on the nature side, uh, William Tryon in the 1940s – he was working with rats, and he had rats run through a maze. And as he watched the rats run through the maze, he noticed *which* rats were good at maze-learning (made few errors, seemed to learn it quickly) and he labeled these *bright* rats, and he put them in *one* cage. And then the other rats that seemed to have a *hard* time with maze-learning and made a lot of errors, and didn't have a very good sense of direction, he labeled those, uh, *dull* rats, and he kept *them* in a separate cage. And then he had these rats *breed separately*, and he found that after a few generations it was very, very *clear* that the bright rats were producing bright rat *babies*, and the dull rats were producing *dull* rat children, and, um, so Tryon said that this was *conclusive*, uh, that, that intelligence is inherited, an inheritable trait.

Um, human twin studies have also shown us that there's a significant, uh, genetic influence on intelligence. We know that the correlation of IQ scores for identical twins that are raised together in the same environment is about point eight five, which is *very*, very significant. And, uh, even though, uh, even identical twins who are raised *apart*, in *different* environments, uh, identical twins who share exactly the same DNA, but *not* the same environment, still have an IQ correlation of point seven two, which again *is* significant. Fraternal twins, who in terms of DNA are like regular siblings but who tend to share a more similar environment, uh, because of the, the *age* similarity, their correlation is point six. Um. Siblings who are raised together, the correlation is about point four five. So, what we see with those correlations is the more shared DNA that two people have together, uh, the more likely it *is* that they'll also have a similar IQ score.

The relationship is, is not perfect, however. If it was, then the correlation between identical twins, whether they were raised together *or apart*, should be at *one*. And, uh, we don't see that. We see this, um, lower correlation, which tells us that, uh, it has to be, there have to be some environmental factors or some other factors to account for the difference in IQ scores.

Um, *adoption* studies also show us that there's a genetic, uh, contribution to IQ. *Adopted* children have IQ scores which are more like their biological parents' than their *adoptive* parents'. So that's further evidence for, uh, the *nature* view of intelligence.

Narrator: Now complete the steps in your book.

Narrator: Chapter 6, Accounting for Variations in Intelligence
Page 83
Listening for specific information, Step 2

Lecturer: Um, on the nurture side, we have another rat study. Um, Hebbe, that's H-E-B-B-E, who was a contemporary of Tryon's – he worked with rats, and what he did was he raised them in different environments. He, uh, took one group of rats, and he raised them in an enriched environment – lots of things to do, toys, and lots of stimulation for the rats – while *another* group of rats was raised in an *impoverished* environment – nothing to do, bare walls, no, um, no toys to play with, uh, pretty boring for them. And then, uh, he looked at these rats' brains after a period of time, and he found a very *clear* difference in their brain development. The rats that were raised in the *enriched* environment – they had larger, heavier brains than the rats raised in the impoverished environment – their brains were smaller; they were lighter. And the implication here is that the environment, uh, affects the quality of the brain, and this is evidence for the *nurture* view of intelligence.

We've also found in studies with *kids*, when we take disadvantaged, inner-city kids and put them in middle-class suburban homes where education is *valued*, after a period of time, we tend to see a *jump* in IQ of about fifteen points, uh, over the IQs of similar kids that are raised by their own parents, in, uh, in a more impoverished, inner-city environment.

Um, another little piece of support for the *nurture* view comes from a researcher named Robert Zajonc. Ah, that's spelled Z-A-J-O-N-C. Um, Zajonc has come up with something called the *confluence model of intelligence*. It's a fact that older-born, oldest-born children have IQ scores that are higher than their younger siblings', and Zajonc's confluence model offers an explanation for that. It, it says that the child's intelligence is formed by the intellectual climate in which the child is raised, which *he* measures as the average IQ.

So, let's take an example. Uh, if, if you take the case of two adults who, uh, just get married, OK? And let's say that they're of normal intelligence. So, now a little kid comes along – they have a baby – and that baby doesn't add anything to the intellectual climate of the home; he's lowering the average family IQ. OK, and now you have *another* kid a few years *later*, and now, now the home is becoming *even* more child-centered, so the intellectual climate is, uh, the average IQ of the *home* gets lower and lower with each successive child. So, how can parents avoid this problem? Zajonc says the way to avoid this is to space out the birth of your children as far as you can, and that keeps the intellectual climate of the house at a more adult level.

Uh, now, in a later study, Zajonc concluded that the confluence model is at best only one of the many factors that could be contributing to differences on IQ tests. And there's been a lot of research on other factors that could affect a child's intellectual development – factors like, uh, increased TV viewing, uh, drug use, food additives, um, decrease in funding for schools. Uh, we also don't know the effects of single parenting, and two-career families, and day care – that's yet to be determined. So, there's still a lot of research to be done on the development of intelligence.

Narrator: Now complete the steps in your book. This is the end of Chapter 6. The program continues on the next cassette.

7

Narrator: Cassette 4.
Chapter 7, Body Language
Page 87
Reading nonverbal cues, Step 2

Woman: You are going to hear eight statements. In your book, find the gesture that expresses each statement. Write the number of the correct drawing in the blank after the letter.
a. Bye, bye!
b. Ummm, *sort* of.
c. Come here.
d. I don't know.
e. She's crazy!
f. Good job.
g. Oh, about this tall.
h. Wish me good luck!

Narrator: Now complete the steps in your book.

Narrator: Chapter 7, Body Language
Page 89
Answering true/false questions, Step 2

Interviewer: Marcos, how many years have you lived in the United States?
Marcos: Ah, I was a student here for about five years, and then I, uh, went back and lived in Brazil for a while, and then I moved back in 1991.
Interviewer: OK, and what I wanted to pick your brain about was, um, *body language* and things that you might remember noticing when you came here – things that North Americans do differently from people in Brazil, um, for example, eye contact. Is that something you noticed?
Marcos: Um, well, you know, there *is* a big difference. I've learned that North Americans are *much* more . . . How can I say this? It's very important for them to have, uh, your eye contact so that they know that you're with them in the conversation, that you're paying attention, and so forth. And what I've noticed about myself is that my eyes tend to, uh, wander in the distance and go to other places, and

I've had people think that I wasn't paying attention–
Interviewer: Yeah?
Marcos: But I was just trying to focus.
Interviewer: Trying to focus. That's interesting. Uh, what about hand movements? Have you noticed a difference between Brazilians and Americans?
Marcos: Well, that's interesting. A part of my family in Brazil – well, these are people who were part of my *first* wife's family – and they were from Italy–
Interviewer: Uh-huh.
Marcos: And, uh, they talked with their hands *a lot*, and *we* had always noticed it, y'know, but we never thought that *we* did the same *thing*, uh, as Brazilians.
Interviewer: Oh!
Marcos: But on observing, uh, how much, uh, people do not make *gestures* here, I have become more aware of the fact that Brazilians *indeed* talk a lot with their hands.
Interviewer: Uh-huh! Well, what about the *kinds* of gestures we use, I mean, to signal certain things. Have you ever completely misunderstood a situation because of an unfamiliar gesture?
Marcos: Well, y'know, a case comes to mind. This was when my wife and I were living in Brazil, and we–
Interviewer: Now, your wife's North American, is that right?
Marcos: Yes, she is. And we were at a party one day at school, and we were standing quite, uh, far apart from each other, and she put out her right arm and started opening and closing her fing-, *hand*, and in Brazil, that, what that means is "Come closer." So I kept coming closer, and she turned around and, and walked away and I was very confused. And later I asked her, "Why did you keep calling me if you didn't want to talk to me?" And she said, "I wasn't doing any such thing!"
Interviewer: Hah!
Marcos: So I repeated the gesture to her and what she meant to do was, was kinda *wave* at me, but that's not the way *Brazilians* wave. But it must've been very funny to the students that were

watching because I kept walking towards her and she kept walking away.

Narrator: Now complete the steps in your book.

Narrator: **Chapter 7, Body Language**
Page 89
Answering true/false questions,
Step 2, Page 90

Interviewer: SunRan, let me just ask, first of all, how long have you been in the United States?

SunRan: Ten years.

Interviewer: Ten years. OK, well, uh, can I ask you, are there any American hand signals that gave you trouble when you first came to the United States?

SunRan: Well, yeah! The way you say "come . . ." we do that kind of hand signal for a dog, not for people.

Interviewer: Oh! With your palm upward? That's for calling dogs in Korea?

SunRan: Yeah. And another one – when older Koreans are pointing, they, um, sometimes use their middle finger instead of their index finger.

Interviewer: *Really!* I didn't know that.

SunRan: Yeah, so my dad still does that, and it can sometimes kind of cause trouble.

Interviewer: I bet! Uh, what about eye contact? Is that different in Korea? Is it, is it OK for people to look at each other directly?

SunRan: Well, not a higher-level person. I mean, if I talk to my boss or to an older person, I should look at his mouth or chin, not in his eyes.

Interviewer: Really!

SunRan: And boys and girls – if they look in each other's eyes, it means they are interested.

Interviewer: Oh! So you shouldn't look at someone if you're not interested!

SunRan: No.

Interviewer: Are there any other differences in body language that you've noticed?

SunRan: Um, I find Americans tend to make a lot of facial expressions when they talk.

Interviewer: Oh.

SunRan: I think Koreans use less body language when they communicate.

Interviewer: Oh.

SunRan: They kind of stand still, sit still, try not to move anything.

Interviewer: Now, is that true for men *and* women?

SunRan: That's both men and women.

Interviewer: Well–

Interviewer: In Korea long ago, when you moved your body a lot, it kind of, um, meant you were bad-mannered.

Interviewer: Well, that's interesting. Now you've been here for ten years. Have you changed? Do you use your arms more now than . . . when you're talking? Or your hands?

SunRan: I use my arms and hands a lot – a lot of body language. Yes, I do.

Interviewer: More than, than you would if you were speaking Korean?

SunRan: Right. And when I go to Korea, I try to minimize that. Especially when I talk to my relatives. They kind of tell me, "How, how come you move so much? How come you don't sit still?"

Narrator: Now complete the steps in your book.

Narrator: **Chapter 7, Body Language**
Page 90
Restating what you have heard,
Step 2

Interviewer: Airi, let's see, how long have you been here?

Airi: Nine months.

Interviewer: OK, and you came here with your husband, who's American.

Airi: Yes, he's American.

Interviewer: So, I just, I wanted to ask you if you've ever had any misunderstandings because of differences in gestures that Americans use, or maybe eye contact, or–

Airi: Ah, yes. I had an experience when I, uh, participated in my husband's sister's wedding. Wedding day, we took a picture–

Interviewer: Uh-huh?

Airi: Like a family picture?

Interviewer: Yeah?

Airi: Like a, like a formal picture? This is it.

Interviewer: Oh! You have it here!

Airi: Uh, like everyone is *smiling* with, uh, open mouths.

Interviewer: Yeah! *Teeth* showing!

Airi: Yeah, except me. And after I received this picture, I felt really embarrassed.

Interviewer: Huh!

Airi: His mother asked me, "Why didn't you smile?" So I said to her, uh, "I *smiled*!" Like Japanese way.

Interviewer: "I *am* smiling!" Yeah! So it's just a cultural difference.

Airi: Yeah. In Japan, in this situation, like a formal picture–

Interviewer: Uh-huh.

Airi: We usually just make a smile, but we don't open our mouth.

Interviewer: Hmm! Let me ask you about eye contact. I've heard that too much eye contact in Japan is a bad thing. Is that true?

Airi: Well, I, I don't think . . . it's not bad in Japan.

Interviewer: So people look at each other?

Airi: I think it's good in Japan also – good to look at each other.

Interviewer: OK.

Airi: Like really listening to each other, really trying to understand.

Interviewer: Hmm! Are there *any* differences in eye contact that you've noticed between Japan and the U.S.?

Airi: No, I think almost the same.

Interviewer: Any other differences that you've noticed?

Airi: Like, uh, American *teachers* use more, like, a body language, like, uh–

Interviewer: Like that? Like the sign for "so-so?" Just like moving your hand to show "so-so, sort of."

Airi: Yeah.

Interviewer: So *gestures*–

Airi: Different gestures. We don't have like this in Japan.

Interviewer: Uh-huh.

Airi: Yeah.

Interviewer: So the gestures are *different* but there are also *more* of them. In Japan you don't use your hands so much?

Airi: Yeah. Not like Americans. Less. But I think *I* use *a lot*. I use my hands a lot.

Interviewer: More than typical?

Airi: Yeah, because since I started dating my husband, we can't communicate very well – we couldn't – so I wanted him to *try* to understand–

Interviewer: Yeah!

Airi: So use hands for everything.

Interviewer: You used everything you could! I understand!

Airi: *"Please, please understand!!"*

Narrator: Now complete the steps in your book.

Narrator: **Chapter 7, Body Language**
Page 95
Note taking: Mapping, Step 2

Lecturer: Maybe we should begin by mentioning an obvious one and that's what we call body language, that is, what we are saying by our posture, the way in which we hold ourselves; our gestures, uh, that is, use of our hands; our facial expressions – all the things that say something to the other person, *not* through words, but simply by how we present ourselves, how we move. Uh, our *eye contact*, for example, is one that we may not think of right away, but, uh, it's *extremely* important, and our tone of *voice*. And how about the meaning of touch? Touch communication, that is, who has permission to touch whom and under what circumstances.

Narrator: Now complete the steps in your book.

Narrator: **Chapter 7, Body Language**
Page 96
Mapping, Step 2

Lecturer: OK. Uh, today we're going to begin our discussion of *nonverbal* communication. Now, experts in the field of communication estimate that somewhere between sixty and ninety percent of everything we communicate is nonverbal. Uh, how can that possibly be true? After all, we put so much emphasis on our words when we're trying to communicate something. We think about what we want to say, uh. We worry about what we *didn't* say. We, uh, we think about what we *should* have said. I mean, we're concerned about how the other person interprets our words, and we interpret the *other* person's words. So, there's enormous emphasis in all our interactions on *words*. What about this sixty to ninety percent that is supposedly *non*verbal? What does that *mean* exactly?

OK, uh, let me ask you to *think* about some of the ways in which you communicate nonverbally – just the broad areas. Maybe we should begin by mentioning an obvious one and that's what we call *body language*, that is, what we are saying by our *posture*, the way in which we hold ourselves; our *gestures*, uh, that is, use of our hands; our *facial expressions* – all the things that say something to the other person, *not* through words, but simply by how we present ourselves, how we move. Uh, let's see, our *eye contact*, for example, is one that we may not think of right away, but, it's *extremely* important, and *our tone of voice*. And how about the meaning of *touch*? Touch communication, that is, who has permission to touch whom and under what circumstances.

A very important point that I'd like to make is that nonverbal communication is difficult *enough* to study and understand in one's *own* culture, but it becomes *extremely* complicated when we are trying to understand how nonverbal communication functions in an*other* culture, that is, one we're unfamiliar with. I mean, after all, if we're learning about another culture and learning the language of that culture, another language, what do we learn but words – the meaning of words and how they fit together and the pronunciation of words. So that, uh, when we learn, uh, French, we can take our dictionary and look up "fromage," or when we learn German, we can find out what "Käse" is. But there's no dictionary of nonverbal

communication. So, where do we find out what, uh, a certain toss of a head means? Or a certain blink of the eye? Or, uh, the physical distance between people? And it's very easy to misinterpret these cues or to miss them altogether. If you're puzzled by what's happening to you in, in a foreign culture, it's probably the nonverbals that are causing the communication problem.

Narrator: Now complete the steps in your book.

Narrator: **Chapter 7, Body Language**
Page 97
Mapping, Step 2, Page 98

Lecturer: So, the nonverbals are probably responsible for most cross-cultural confusion. Um, let's see, let me give you one or two examples of how this can happen. Uh, a simple one is with eye contact. Americans tend to think that looking *directly* into another person's eye is, is, um, is *appropriate*, and that if you look away or look down, you may be avoiding responsibility, or, um, or, or showing disrespect. And, and this is considered to be *negative*. We learn to "look me straight in the eye!" Look me *straight* in the eye. Now in, um, in some other cultures, it's a sign of disrespect to look at another person straight in the eye. In Japan, for example, there's *much* less direct eye contact than in the United States. So, something as simple as that can cause great confusion.

Ah, to give another cross-cultural example from Japan, I can tell you that when I first began working in Japan, I was, oh boy, I was awfully confused because I was paying attention to what was *said* to me rather than to the nonverbal cues. We have a study-abroad program and when I was dealing with my Japanese colleagues, I would often ask questions, um, you know, that had to do with the program for our students. And I would ask one particular colleague if we could make certain changes.

Now, uh, I have great respect for this colleague, and I know that he wanted to cooperate. There were times when I would ask him things like, um, for instance, "Can we, um, um, ah, allow students in the dormitory to stay out later at night?" And *often* the response I would get *verbally* was that maybe we *could* do that, and I always interpreted this as a *green* light, as a strong possibility, because "maybe" for me verbally means "Maybe! Yes! Probably! Let's find a way!" After all, he hadn't said "no."

What I didn't understand was that for my *colleague*, who didn't want to embarrass me by saying, *saying*, *speaking* the word "no" directly – which, which would be considered impolite in *his* culture – he was telling me "no" by saying "maybe" and giving me other cues with his *body* language, and I had to learn to recognize what those cues were. Well, can you imagine what they might be, for example? Well, I started to realize that it had to do with *how* he said "maybe," it had to do with his *tone*: whether he said "Well, maybe!" meaning "Maybe yes!" or "maybe" meaning "maybe *not*." It had to do with, perhaps, whether he looked embarrassed, or whether he looked uncomfortable when he said that, or whether he seemed excited about the idea, or not. Or, or maybe how he, his posture, his body posture, how he held himself. I had to start *observing* those things.

Now, I'll admit to you that it's still very difficult for me because I don't understand the nonverbal cues in Japanese society as well as I might understand them here in my own culture. But now I'm much more aware that I have to pay attention to them and that I have to learn to observe more carefully. And you know what? That's probably the most important lesson of nonverbal

communication – that is, that we *have to* pay attention, to observe closely, what is happening *both* in our *own* patterns of communication *and* in those of the people around us, and that this really deserves our study and our attention. I, I mean, it's not only extremely interesting, but it's so important if we want to understand the more *hidden* side of communication.

Narrator: Now complete the steps in your book. This is the end of Chapter 7. Now please fast-forward to the end of this side and turn over the cassette to continue.

Narrator: **Chapter 8, The Language of Touch, Space, and Artifacts**
Page 101
Listening to directions, Step 1

Woman: Look at the pictures. Listen to each message and in the blank write the number of the picture that seems to match it best.
a. I'm in *love* with you.
b. I'm rich and sophisticated.
c. I want to protect you.
d. I'm conservative and dependable.
e. You're a stranger.
f. I'm different.
g. I'm independent and I love adventure.
h. You're my friend.

Narrator: Now complete the steps in your book.

Narrator: **Chapter 8, The Language of Touch, Space, and Artifacts**
Page 103
Summarizing what you have heard, Step 2

Interviewer: Marcos, do Brazilians stand close together when they're talking?
Marcos: Oh, much closer than North Americans, yeah. Yeah, I've had several experiences. One time when I was in a classroom, I had somebody,

um, else that I was talking to, a *student* of mine, and I kept – um, a gentleman from Korea – and I kept getting closer to him, and he kept backing up.

Interviewer: Oh, dear.

Marcos: And I didn't really notice what was going on until I saw this, this look of *total despair* on his face, and I realized that he had backed up the whole length of the classroom and now we were in one corner of the room.

Interviewer: Really?

Marcos: He looked very uncomfortable, and I had obviously, uh, invaded his body bubble, his *space*.

Interviewer: Yeah! Huh. How about *touch*? Do Brazilians touch each other more than North Americans?

Marcos: Yes, in Brazil it's really common for people who are talking to you to stand really close and to touch you often, or to put their arm around you, or something, depending on who it is.

Interviewer: Now this is male/female?

Marcos: Uh, let's see, uh, yes, male and female, uh, but I also think it's not uncommon for male friends to, uh, touch each other, say, to put an arm around the shoulder or something.

Interviewer: Uh-huh. Do you find, have you found that you've *modified* your bubble, your space, to accommodate us cold North Americans? Do you stand farther away from people now? And maybe not touch people as much?

Marcos: Yes, and I, uh, think it's a partly unconscious process – you just modify. I mean, if you *don't*, then, uh, when you're standing in line you get too close to people, uh, and then, uh, they turn around and they stare.

Interviewer: Yeah.

Marcos: So, uh, *yeah*, I feel that I have had to *enlarge* my bubble–

Interviewer: Yeah.

Marcos: And, and stand, uh, a little *farther*, uh, than I would. And, and I've noticed in my family *too*, you know, I've noticed that when we lived in Brazil, we were more, uh, physical, or walked more

closely or touched more often in public, than we do here.

Interviewer: Interesting.

Marcos: I think especially between my wife and me this has happened because it's when one looks around and there aren't very many people touching each other in public, then one feels a little self-conscious.

Interviewer: SunRan, have you noticed big differences in how people touch in the U.S.?

SunRan: Well, one big difference is shaking hands. Men and women in Korea don't shake hands, but I learned to do that when I came here.

Interviewer: Uh-huh.

SunRan: So when I went back to visit Korea, I forgot and I tried to shake hands, and they don't do that. So I was kind of embarrassed.

Interviewer: Do people in Korea touch at all in public?

SunRan: Well, in Korea we kinda tend to show more affection to the same sex than the opposite sex.

Interviewer: I see.

SunRan: So, like, if I have a girlfriend, I kind of walk around hand in hand or arm in arm.

Interviewer: Uh-huh?

SunRan: Yeah, I did that a lot in Korea, but I cannot do it here.

Interviewer: Uh-huh.

SunRan: That's something different. And men and women show a lot more affection here than in Korea.

Interviewer: Men and women?

SunRan: Yeah.

Interviewer: Is it wrong in Korea for a man and woman to touch each other in public?

SunRan: You're not supposed to!

Interviewer: Ah, interesting. Even if they're married?

SunRan: Yeah. You know, the first thing that kinda was a real shock to me when I came here was kids, high school kids – they *hug* and *kiss* at school. That was a *real* shock to me.

Interviewer: Hmm!

SunRan: And the little boys and girls – they have their first kiss when they are six or seven, like that. That's strange too because we never, *never* do anything like that until, until when you're older, maybe twenties.

Interviewer: Airi, what about differences that you might have noticed in space or in how Americans touch each other?

Airi: Yeah, I think many Japanese, uh, have the same opinion about hugging.

Interviewer: Yeah?

Airi: Hugging and kissing. In Japan at the beginning of our relationship . . . my husband?

Interviewer: Yeah?

Airi: He was confused because my family never hugged him and, uh, or kiss, not kiss especially. My mother never, never touched him or, you know, so he worried, "Maybe she doesn't love me."

Interviewer: Interesting!

Airi: Yeah, and also he can't, uh, he couldn't communicate with her very well. So, so he felt really confused and nervous.

Interviewer: Yeah, cuz in America, you know, if you can't talk, you can at least put your arm on someone to show them–

Airi: Yeah! Show love–

Interviewer: Communicate that way. Huh. So, you say your parents didn't hug or kiss *him*. Did they hug or kiss *you*? I mean, within your family, do, in Japan do people hug each other? Like, did your mother hug *you*?

Airi: No, I think never! When I was a child, maybe she did–

Interviewer: Yeah.

Airi: But no. Just communicate by words. Sometimes shake hands but not hug.

Interviewer: Huh.

Airi: Now I can understand my husband's feeling.

Interviewer: Uh-huh.

Airi: Since I came here, I understand his feeling because my American family always hugs – hug and kiss – and at first I felt really, really confused but little by little I felt more love or affection for them.

Interviewer: Uh-huh.

Airi: I feel really comfortable about that.

Interviewer: So, now do you hug and it's OK?

Airi: Yeah, yeah! I really like it!

Narrator: Now complete the steps in your book.

Narrator: **Chapter 8, The Language of Touch, Space, and Artifacts**
Page 104
Listening for specific information, Step 2

Interviewer: Airi, I wanted to ask you about the way Americans dress – their sort of fashion sense, maybe. What differences have you noticed between your country and the U.S.?

Airi: It's, uh, just one word – *casual*.

Interviewer: Yeah?

Airi: A lot more casual. Like, uh, Japanese are a lot more . . . have to *care*, ah–

Interviewer: Yeah, they're more, uh, careful.

Airi: Yeah.

Interviewer: About, about what they . . . how they look?

Airi: Yeah.

Interviewer: Is it, is it a *status*, uh, thing? Y'know, where you hafta have, um, will people think *badly* of you if you–

Airi: Yeah! We always think about other people's opinion, I think.

Interviewer: So, um, things like wearing *brand* names, y'know, like wearing designer labels–

Airi: Yeah.

Interviewer: That is important?

Airi: Yeah, and, uh, and, uh, always think about what is popular recently.

Interviewer: So, you have to wear something that's in fashion now.

Airi: Yeah.

Interviewer: Is that, do most people feel that way? Both men and women?

Airi: Not so, especially young people.

Interviewer: Both men and women?

Airi: Yeah.

Interviewer: Whereas Americans, some of them are concerned about fashion, but it's sort of a matter of choice. If they don't care, it's OK.

Airi: Yeah! Yeah! I like, uh, watching American people because they're different. Each person is really different.

Interviewer: Yeah!

Airi: They have, uh, more, um, identity.

Interviewer: Identity! Individual identity, yeah?

Airi: Yeah. They show that "This is my way" through their clothes.

Interviewer: But in Japan you don't want to do that?

Airi: Yeah. Some *young* people wear strange clothes, but usually you care about other people – you wanna look the same. One example – when Japanese people get married, it's like a fashion show. With a wedding *consultant*?

Interviewer: A consultant, yeah?

Airi: And the bride changes three times – usually, first a white dress, then a kimono, and then a cocktail dress. American wedding system is more personal, I think. More *creative*?

Interviewer: Oh!

Airi: Yeah. More like a, uh, more original. They choose their own colors. Like, uh, for the bridesmaids' dresses, the bride usually chooses the dress color. But in Japan–

Interviewer: You hire somebody. . . . You hire a consultant.

Airi: Yeah, so not so much individual expression.

Interviewer: Hmm.

Narrator: Now complete the steps in your book.

Narrator: **Chapter 8, The Language of Touch, Space, and Artifacts**
Page 107
Note taking: Listening for stress and intonation, Step 2, Page 109

Narrator: Stop the tape after each beep and mark your answers.
One.

Lecturer: How much is conveyed through *verbal* communication? *More* often than *not*, our intense emotions are conveyed *nonverbally*.

Narrator: Two.

Lecturer: Most of our *intense* emotions are expressed through *gestures*, *body position*, *facial expression*, *vocal cues*, *eye contact*, *use* of *space*, and *touching*.

Narrator: Three.

Lecturer: Imagine what would happen if you don't understand this bubble. What might you experience? Possibly *discomfort*, *irritation*, maybe even *anger*.

Narrator: Four.

Lecturer: It could express *affection*, *anger*, *playfulness*, *control*, *status* – these are just a *few* functions of touch.

Narrator: Five.

Lecturer: In *some* cultures, it is common to see same-sex friends holding hands in public. However, think about this behavior in some *other* cultures. Is it appropriate?

Narrator: Now complete the steps in your book.

Narrator: **Chapter 8, The Language of Touch, Space, and Artifacts**
Page 110
Summarizing what you have heard, Step 2

Lecturer: Today we're going to start looking at nonverbal language. Nonverbal communication has often been referred to as the "hidden dimension" of communication. Sometimes this dimension is *so* subtle that we do not even recognize the ways it shapes what we're saying or how people interpret our meaning. In fact, when you think about it, think of some of the emotions that you express in everyday life, like happiness, joy, sadness, and anger, irritation. How much of those expressions are conveyed through verbal communication? More often than not, our *intense* emotions are conveyed *nonverbally* through gestures, body position, facial expression, vocal cues, eye contact, use of space, and touching.

OK. Now, let me make two points about how *nonverbal* communication functions. One is, sometimes when we communicate, it may *only* be through the nonverbal cues. The nonverbal gesture carries *all* our meaning. But, secondly, nonverbal cues also function to help us *interpret* the verbal message, and this is the point I want to focus on first – um, that nonverbal cues help *interpret*, uh, a verbal message. Where we see this *really* in a *very* subtle way is through the use of humor and sarcasm. Y'know, in humor and sarcasm, the verbal message – y'know, what is actually said – is only a small part of the message. It's often the *non*verbal cues that signal: "Hey, how's this message to be taken, seriously or not? I mean, do they really mean it, or are they joking?"

Take, for example, when an American sees a new style of clothing which they may not like – how they might signal that they don't like it. Well, they might say, "Oh, *that's* a good look." OK? Now, if you're from a different culture, how do you know if they really mean it, or if they're being sarcastic and they really mean the opposite? Well, it's very difficult because it's the *non*verbal cues – *not* the words – that are carrying the meaning here. It's usually the tone of *voice* or a facial expression. I guess this is why a lot of international students often tell me that it's humor that's the *most* difficult part of American culture to understand. And, similarly, when Americans go abroad.

There's another area of nonverbal communication that is often overlooked, and in this case the nonverbal gesture carries all the meaning – and that is *proxemics*. That's P-R-O-X-E-M-I-C-S. Proxemics refers to our personal space. Y'know, the anthropologist Edward Hall calls this personal space of ours our "body bubbles." Body bubbles are interesting because they're very subtle. You hardly ever recognize them until someone pops your bubble. In other words, when somebody comes too close, or violates your private space, you are suddenly *conscious* – you become conscious of the bubble. So, what do you do when someone pops your bubble? Do you feel uncomfortable? Do you move away? Do you turn your position? Do you put your books in front of you? Do you suddenly close your jacket? We

always, we tend to adapt our body position when our bubbles get invaded. We see this in crowded elevators, for example.

Um, body bubbles are influenced by many factors: How intimate is the relationship? What is the social context – a party or a bus? Uh, what's the gender relationship? However a strong influence on body bubbles is culture. Um, for example, in Latin American and Middle Eastern cultures, the kind of conversational space, the space between two people just engaged in everyday conversations, is relatively very close compared to Asian and American cultures. Imagine what would happen if you don't *understand* this bubble. What might you experience? Possibly discomfort, irritation, maybe even anger.

Narrator: Now complete the steps in your book.

Narrator: Chapter 8, The Language of Touch, Space, and Artifacts
Page 111
Summarizing what you have heard, Step 2

Lecturer: And a third area of nonverbal communication, an area that's extremely powerful, where there are very strong norms – um, that's kind of social, um, unspoken social rules – strong norms that are easily violated is the area of *touching*. Touch is one of the most sensitive areas of nonverbal communication because touch is never neutral. Take the case of, um, shaking hands with someone. We never think of shaking hands as a form of touch; it seems almost like a ritual. But, in fact, it's one of the *major* forms of touch between strangers. Now, in American culture, for example, we value *firm* handshakes. I mean, if the handshake is weak and limp, we might say, "He or she shakes hands like a fish."

Touch is really amazing. It's very subtle and complex. Think for a moment about some of the functions of touch. Uh, what could it express?

Well, it could express affection, anger, playfulness, control, status. . . . These are just a *few* functions of touch.

Two major influences on touching behavior – think about your body bubbles again – one is *gender*, and the other is *culture*. We can see both influences – of gender and of culture – when we contrast same-sex touching – this'd be touching between two men or between two women. Uh, in some cultures, it is common to see same-sex friends holding hands and embracing in public. This behavior is not interpreted as sexual. However, think about this behavior in some other cultures. Is it appropriate? Could it be taboo? I recall my own surprise. I remember when I was visiting in China and, uh, I would see young men holding hands in the streets, and young women also. And at *first* I was surprised, but I thought it was, y'know, very *affectionate*, very *warm*. So I decided that I was going to incorporate the *same* habit when I came back to the United States. So my sister and I started to, uh, hold *hands* in *public*. But we felt very awkward about it, and we stopped doing it.

So, you see the norms for touching are *very* powerful. Uh, they're easy to violate and, as I discovered, they're difficult to change. That is why it is *very* important to understand what is appropriate touch and what is taboo in another culture.

Last, I think we have to remember that even misinterpretations and confusion in nonverbal communication don't always end in, uh, serious misinterpretations, or anger, or alienation. They're oftentimes the source of a lot of humor, a lot of laughter, and a lot of camaraderie between people of different cultures.

Narrator: Now complete the steps in your book. This is the end of Chapter 8. The program continues on the next cassette.

9

Narrator: Cassette 5.
Chapter 9, Friendship
Page 115
Listening for specific information, Step 1

Man: Listen as each person gives the name of a good friend. Draw a line from the first column to the second column to connect their names. Then write down when and where they met.

Interviewer: Otis, can you tell me the name of one of your good friends?

Otis: Gee, that's difficult! I have so many good friends.

Interviewer: OK, tell me one.

Otis: OK, uh, Tom.

Interviewer: And when and where did you meet him?

Otis: Uh, at Yale after World War II – that was 1946. We were in the same class and we had a lot of interests in common, like music, uh . . .

Interviewer: David, who is one of your best friends?

David: Uh, let's say Douglas.

Interviewer: And where did you meet him?

David: In college – we were both studying music.

Interviewer: And when was that?

David: Uh, let's see 1968.

Interviewer: Pam, can you name a good friend of yours?

Pam: Uh, one of my best friends is Jeanette.

Interviewer: And when and how did you get to be friends?

Pam: Um, oh back in 1967, I think, when we were in grade school. We were both social outcasts.

Interviewer: Yeah?

Pam: Yeah, we were both terrible at sports.

Interviewer: Tony, can you tell me the name of one of your best friends?

Tony: Uh, Hubert.

Interviewer: And how did you meet him?

Tony: We met in college. We were in classes together, and we just got to be good friends.

Interviewer: How long ago was this?

Tony: How long? Um, Oh! Twenty-seven years!

Interviewer: Catherine, who would you say is one of your good friends?

Catherine: Uh, Odette.

Interviewer: OK, Odette. And when and where did you meet her?

Catherine: Uh, I met her in graduate school. And that was, let's see, 1985.

Interviewer: Ruth, who's one of your best friends?

Ruth: Oh! Well, the first person that comes to mind is Esther.

Interviewer: How did you get to be friends?

Ruth: Well, I met her in 1982 at my synagogue. I already knew about her from another friend, and when I met her, I just knew I wanted to be friends.

Narrator: Now complete the steps in your book.

Narrator: Chapter 9, Friendship
Page 117
Answering true/false questions,
Step 2

Interviewer: Catherine, how long have you and I been . . . how long have we known each other?

Catherine: Let's see, we met when you interviewed me for a teaching job. Was it six, seven, maybe seven or eight years ago?

Interviewer: Yeah, I guess so. Yeah, that's right.

Catherine: But we began to be *friends*, um, I think it . . . what might've started it was when I asked you a *favor*, which was to help me give my cat, Sophie, a flea bath.

Interviewer: Oh, yes!

Catherine: Yeah. That was, that was hard for me. It was hard for me to ask that kind of favor to someone I didn't know that well cuz, you know, it seemed fairly bothersome, but it it turned out to be kinda *fun*.

Interviewer: Yeah, it *was* fun! I still have the scars.

Catherine: She had a lotta fleas on her.

Interviewer: She had a *lotta* fleas on her, yeah. Well, we, *yeah*, and after that we started to be good friends. One thing that I've realized about you is that you have *a lot* of close friends from,

you know, different periods in your life.

Interviewer: How have your friendships gotten started?

Catherine: Hmm, well, I'd say that most of my friendships have sprung from some kind of a shared *interest*, y'know, either at work or school or somewhere else. I *have* made a lot of friends at work. I value work *a lot*, and I feel like I have a particular work ethic, and so if I'm working with other people who have the *same* work ethic, that, for me, is, is something *very large* that we have in common, it makes for a, um, a good base for a possible friendship. Or sometimes it's just that I have some, I don't know, some sense of "Yeah, this is a person that I'd like to get to know" because I heard them make a remark that I thought was funny or I observed them in some situation or we work well together or we have some common interest.

Interviewer: You mentioned your friend Odette earlier. How did you two get to be friends?

Catherine: Oh! Well, let's see, um, I was going to graduate school and I was taking a course in linguistics. And I noticed this other woman in the same class and I *really liked* the way she *looked*, the way, y'know, and I remember thinking, "Oh, she's too cool! She would never wanna be friends with someone like me!" And I didn't talk to her cuz I was just so intimidated by her coolness – oh gosh. And then I think what happened, we were in a study group together and got a chance to talk. At some point she revealed to me that she'd thought I was too cool for her too. And we ended up being great friends. Yeah, and we realized that neither of us was that cool after all.

Narrator: Now complete the steps in your book.

Narrator: Chapter 9, Friendship
Page 118
Summarizing what you have heard, Step 2

Interviewer: Catherine, you have quite a few long distance friendships. How do you maintain them?

Catherine: Yeah, well, friendship *is* very important to me, um, I think friendships need *tending*. I, I put a big value on being *current* with my friends, and that's something that's hard to do long distance. But there *are* friends I have that I *don't* live close to that I *have* managed to stay *very* close to. My friend Odette lives back East, and she's not much for writing letters, so we talk on the phone at least once a week, usually for an hour at a time, and we take turns calling so I stay current with her, um, by *talking*.

Interviewer: So, how are your phone bills?

Catherine: My phone bills are *high*. But, um, I consider it just like one of my living expenses. You know, like rent. And then there's several friends that I *do* write cuz I love to write, and I love to get letters. And, and it's, it's a cool thing cuz I have . . . It's a concrete record of, um, you know, of what we were *doing*.

Interviewer: You save–

Catherine: Yeah, I save all my letters.

Interviewer: Do you re-read them?

Catherine: Y'know, I *don't*. Um, I don't on a regular basis, but something, there's something about throwing away a letter that I just can't do it. And I've got quite a collection. My one friend Doug especially – he likes to write and I've been writing to him for about twenty years now.

Interviewer: Huh!

Catherine: Yeah. We met when we were working at the same place. And then he went to Taiwan for two years and we wrote letters. We didn't know each other all that well, but we got to know each other through letters over the first two years and ever since then we've been good *friends*.

Interviewer: That's nice!

Catherine: *Yeah*, it's, it's *cool*. Although when I first, actually when I first saw him after writing him for two years, I was a *little nervous* that we wouldn't be able to *function* without a pen and paper between us, you know, cuz I didn't . . . I felt like, my *God*, I've never really, I've never spent *time* with this person. I've just said all these things and, he, he knows all my secrets and I know all *his* secrets, but we haven't spent time together. But *it was OK*.

Interviewer: So, some friends you telephone, and others you write to?

Catherine: Oh and *e-mail*! I had *one* friend who just wasn't, you know, just wasn't into writing letters, but she, she got *on-line* and *e-mail is her thing*, and since I've gotten an e-mail address recently, I've discovered, I've heard from her like, uh, twice a week for the past two months which is, which is *unprecedented*. I've *known* her for a long time – since, oh, I'd say, 1980, I think. And we've always considered ourselves friends, but I haven't . . . I've kind of been in and out of touch with her and now I'm, I'm back in good touch with her cuz she'll sit down and write me a letter on e-mail where she just couldn't do it on pen and paper, so that's great! I'm all for e-mail! I just think it's another way to keep in touch.

Interviewer: Yeah. So, in your view what is it that good friends do for each other, Catherine?

Catherine: Well, I think friends . . . I feel like one thing I want *my* friends to do is to call me on things, you know, to let me know if I do something that upsets them for whatever reason. I think that's *one* thing friends, you know, *do* for each other and that's why sometimes friendship can get prickly and *hard*. Um, and you can fight, but I've never, I've never felt fighting was bad. It's just showing that you *care*. But other things, I think friends, um, provide comfort and support and adventure and *jokes*! Especially with old friends. You share *jokes* that you've created together that you've understood and all you have to do is say one word, and the other person can go off into *peals* of laughter and that's, that's pretty, um–

Interviewer: It's powerful.

Catherine: Yeah, it is. And it's a great way to mark time, I think. To realize that you've actually accrued this common-

Interviewer: History!

Catherine: Yeah! I recently e-mailed my friend Corey back in Chicago about a problem I was having in my personal life and, um, he wrote back with making reference to an argument that he and I'd had, like, *ten years ago*. And he still remembered and I still remembered and it was *really funny* and, y'know, I'm sitting there, y'know, and I'm kind of depressed and I read his answer and I just started *laughing* cuz it was, y'know, it was a *joke*. Y'know, he made this joke that was only funny because, because we've known each other for so long, and we have this great history. It's kind of like . . . I think of friends as the family that we get to *choose* and that's, that's why friendship's such a wonderful thing.

Narrator: Now complete the steps in your book.

Narrator: **Chapter 9, Friendship**
Page 121
Note taking: Using morphology, context, and nonverbal cues to guess word meaning, Step 2

Narrator: One.

Lecturer: But it's also rather *subjective*; friendship means very different things to different people.

Narrator: Two.

Lecturer: As a therapist, I'm always thinking about a client's *social network*. When I'm working with a client, it's always critical to take into account that person's *support systems*, and by that I'm talking about family, friends.

Narrator: Three.

Lecturer: You probably know of adults who consider themselves "loners" and say that they are *content* with that condition.

Narrator: Four.

Lecturer: There can be a lot of pain involved with friendship – it's a risky business. When we make friends, or try to make them, we become *vulnerable to* rejection. Each of us probably has a painful childhood memory of being cast aside by one friend in favor of another.

Narrator: Five.

Lecturer: And the senator said, "But what *advice* did you give her?" The woman replied, "Well, I didn't give her any advice; I listened to her." And the senator was *incredulous*. He was *absolutely incredulous*. He said to her, *"Whadda you mean?"*

Narrator: Now complete the steps in your book.

Narrator: **Chapter 9, Friendship**
Page 123
Listening for specific information, Step 2

Lecturer: In some respects friendship seems like a very straightforward topic – everyone wants friends; most of us have friends. But it's also rather subjective; friendship means very different things to different people. What I'll be focusing on today is the importance of friendship to *me*, as an individual and as a psychotherapist, and, uh, then on some differences I have observed in how men and women *view* friendship.

My first memory of consciously contemplating friendship was as a young boy about six or seven years old – in 1963 or '64 – and Barbra Streisand had just come out with her song "People." "People who need people are the luckiest people in the world." My older brother bought the record and played it twenty-four hours a day, and I kept *hearing* it, and I remember thinking: Is that really true? Do we need people? And is it

OK to need people? And, as I've gotten older, more and more I tend to answer that question in the affirmative.

As a therapist, I'm always thinking about a client's social network. Along with sleep patterns and appetite, this is an important indicator of a person's general functioning. When I work with a client who's *suicidal*, it's always critical to take into account that person's support systems, and by that I'm talking about family and friends. Does that person feel supported in the world? Do they have meaningful connections? There are two reasons why I think about that, and the first one is . . . the person who *does* feel supported is *much* less likely to attempt suicide in the first place. Suicide is very often the manifestation of an abject sense of alienation. And second, if a person is suicidal, it's very important to hook them *up* with their support systems so that they can be monitored and, and kept safe. Someone without friends is almost certain to be depressed.

You probably know of adults who consider themselves "loners" and say that they are *content* with that condition. My sense is that while that may in part be true, it's almost always the function of a defense mechanism. There can be a lot of pain involved with friendship – it's a risky business. When we make friends, or try to make them, we become vulnerable to rejection. Each of us probably has a painful childhood memory of being cast aside by one friend in favor of another. And that really hurts. Rejection by friends is especially painful for children.

So, many loners, after repeated rejection, adapt by consciously deciding not to get close to anyone. It's easier that way, and it's less painful. In effect, they're saying, "If I tell you who I am, and you don't like who I am, that's all I've got. So I don't want to take that chance. I don't want to let you know who I really am." And of course it's impossible to form a friendship if you're holding other people at a *distance* like this. To make friends you have to run the risk of being rejected.

Narrator: Now complete the steps in your book.

Narrator: **Chapter 9, Friendship**
Page 124
Listening for specific information, Step 2

Lecturer: Another aspect of my work involving friendship – and one that I find extremely interesting – has to do with the different ways that men and women can have friends. On the whole, women are, are *much* more likely than men to want to get together and talk with each other about what is going on in their lives, about how they're feeling. Men, on the other hand, are usually more comfortable *doing* things with their friends, such as playing basketball or going to a game.

Now, this is a generalization, and it certainly does not apply to all couples. I will say, however, that there are *significant* aspects of this dynamic in well over fifty percent of the couples I work with. And the way that this manifests itself in my office is that I'll find that men and women tend to want *very* different things from one another. Women are much more likely to want to be listened to and to be comforted. And they're not particularly interested in being "fixed." Men, for their part, usually want to *solve*, want to arrive at *solutions* – how can this problem be fixed? And, as is often the case, we treat our *partners* the same way that *we* want to be treated. Men try to fix women and women try to listen to men, which is not what either one is *wanting*. And oftentimes I'll hear something in my office along the lines of "Why can't she just be like my buddies? Y'know, we get along fine."

If you happened to see the

Clarence Thomas – Anita Hill hearings on television, you would have seen this gender difference played out in an extraordinary fashion. Anita Hill accused Clarence Thomas of having sexually harassed her, and then she called a panel of four people to support her testimony. These were people who had known her for years, very respectable people – there was a *judge*, a *lawyer*, a *professor* – and all of them stated that Hill confided in them about the harassment at the time it was happening.

I'll never forget the interchange between one of the women on Hill's panel and one of the senators – a male – who was questioning her. After she told the senators that Hill had told her about the *harassment*, one of the senators asked, "So what did you *do*?" And the woman replied, "I listened to her." And the senator said, "But what *advice* did you give her?" The woman replied, "Well, I didn't give her any advice; I listened to her." And the senator was *incredulous*. He was *absolutely incredulous*. He said to her, "Whadda you mean? She told you that she was being sexually harassed by her boss, and you didn't give her *any* advice about what to do?!" "Well, no, I just *listened* to her."

And I thought, "*That is it!* That's it in a *nutshell*." And other senators asked the same, the same kind of *questions* of her. These guys were *so . . .* How to put it? Um, they're so used to giving advice that they couldn't *fathom* that one friend would *not* give another friend advice in that kind of situation. In fact, they believed it so strongly that many were convinced that Hill's panel members were *lying*, that she'd never spoken to them. I found it a remarkably concise and dramatic snapshot of how *different* men and women can be in how they *view* friendship.

But, whatever it is that we want from our friends – and as I said earlier, friendship means different things to different people – it's a fact that we all *want* and need people in our lives that accept us and love us for who we are. The people we love – and who love us back – are our friends.

Narrator: Now complete the steps in your book. This is the end of Chapter 9. Now please fast-forward to the end of this side and turn over the cassette to continue.

10

Narrator: Chapter 10, Love
Page 128
Listening for details, Step 1

Woman: One.

Les: My name is Les. I'm a librarian. I'm divorced and in my late thirties. I enjoy listening to jazz and going to movies, museums, that kind of thing. I'm looking for someone who kinda likes the same things, I guess.

Speaker: Two.

Michael: My name is Michael. I'm a doctor, and I work very hard. I like to climb mountains in my spare time. I'm thirty-five years old, and I'd like to meet an attractive, younger woman.

Speaker: Three.

Alicia: My name is Alicia. I want to meet a kind, dependable man who will be a good father to my two children, who are four and six years old. I'm a computer engineer.

Speaker: Four.

Frank: My name's Frank. I'm a junior high school teacher. When I'm off in the summer, I love to do gardening and play baseball. I'm thirty-seven years old.

Speaker: Five.

Sara: My name is Sara, and I'm an artist. I'm in my early forties. I guess I'm kind of shy, but I'd like to meet someone I can talk to about art and books, things like that.

Speaker: Six.

Suzanne: I'm Suzanne, and I'm, like, *really* into the healthy lifestyle. I'm in my mid-twenties but I'm looking for a more mature man who makes good money and everything.

Narrator: Now complete the steps in your book.

Narrator: Chapter 10, Love
Page 130
Listening for specific information, Step 2

Interviewer: Ann, how long have you and Jim . . . how long have you been married?

Ann: Thirty-one years, thirty-one years, right? We got married in 1967. December 1967.

Interviewer: Hmm. And that's a long time!

Ann: It *is* a long time.

Interviewer: Um, so I wanted to ask you, how did you initially get interested in each other?

Jim: We met when, uh, I was a senior in college and Ann, uh, was a senior in high school. And she lived in a small town about seven miles from where I was studying, and I was attending the same little country church where she and her family went, and that's how we met.

Ann: Uh-huh.

Interviewer: So, Ann, you were a high school senior.

Ann: That's right – I was sixteen.

Interviewer: Here was this older man!

Ann: I was sixteen years old and I just thought he was the best person I'd ever met in my life. I just fell head over heels in love with him *immediately* at age sixteen. But at age sixteen you usually fall head over heels in love with *a lot of* people. But this one *stuck*, and I had to wait eleven years before he actually proposed and we got married, which is kind of a long time.

Interviewer: Yeah!

Ann: But at age sixteen, I certainly wasn't ready to get married *anyway*. My, one of my *greatest* fears after I met him and decided *pretty* much then and there that he was the man I wanted to marry – but my greatest fear was that he would marry my *sister*, who was three years *older* than I am and therefore more his age, and I was *so relieved* when my sister married someone else.

Interviewer: Now, did Jim give you any encouragement? I mean, eleven years, that's a long time to wait.

Ann: *Verrrrry little.*

Interviewer: Well, Jim, uh, were you as interested in Ann from the beginning as she was in *you*?

Jim: Yes, I was, but I wasn't very good at *showing* it, I think, sometimes. And I really, I really realized after I finished medical school and I was doing my internship out in Seattle–

Ann: Now this was ten years after we met.

Jim: That I, there was a big hole in my life, and I realized what that hole was – that I didn't have, didn't have *Ann* with me, and so I came to New York while Ann was getting her master's degree at Columbia. She'd just come back from two years in the Peace Corps in Ethiopia. And, uh, I brought many pictures of Seattle to show her cuz I understood she was considering a job in Philadelphia – teaching – when she finished. So, I brought all these pictures of Seattle – what a beautiful place it is – and, to encourage her that this was where she should come and, uh–

Interviewer: A rather oblique proposal!

Jim: Kind of oblique. But then the next spring I was visiting back in New York and I got a call from this wonderful older lady in our church – *Aunt Amy* was her name – and Aunt Amy called up and she said, "If you're really interested in that *Ann*, you'd better get yourself down here cuz she might go off and marry one of the *Peace Corps* people she worked with."

Ann: *That's true.*

Jim: Well, I got right in the car and I drove sixty-seven miles down to her home and I asked her mother – her father had died some years before – and I asked her mother for permission to–

Ann: This is true!

Jim: To have Ann's hand and, uh, she was very–

Ann: *She was very happy!*

Jim: Very pleased. And then I proposed to Ann!

Interviewer: And Ann was very happy!

Ann: Ann was very happy!

Jim: And *I* was very happy!

Interviewer: Yeah!

Ann: It was a long time coming, but it was very much worth the wait. But I *realize* that there were several times when I came *very* close to marrying someone else, and I, I feel very fortunate that I, that I–

Interviewer: Yeah! That you waited.

Ann: Yeah!

Narrator: Now complete the steps in your book.

Narrator: Chapter 10, Love
Page 131
Listening for specific information,
Step 2

Jim: I think one of, one of the really nice things about, uh, about our relationship and our, our marriage has been that from the very *beginning* it never was all *me* or all *Ann*. There were, there were so many things that we had both done. Whenever we went out, it'd be, "Well, tell me about the time you went looking for elephants in Ethiopia," and she would remember something that, to ask me to tell friends, and we were both proud of what each other had done, so it wasn't a one-sided kind of thing. And that's, that's been the way it's been through the thirty years, too. I think that both of us have been not only husband and wife but also best friends. And, uh, proud of each other.

Ann: Um-huh! And we share a lot of, a lot of interests. I think that's one of, one of the things that's made our marriage very, very strong.

Interviewer: What interests, for example?

Ann: Well, classical music. We love going to concerts.

Jim: Cross-cultural living – learning the history and learning some of the language – and, uh, we've worked in places all over the world.

Ann: And we both *love* outdoors and gardening, walking. We both come from very strong, very loving families, and our families are very important to us. And, um, our faith is very important to us, our involvement in our church, uh, and just the way we see people and the way we like people to be treated, and caring for others and that kind of thing.

Interviewer: Uh-huh. Are there . . . in what way do you think you *complement* each other? I mean, do you have *differences* that work to your advantage?

Jim: Ann, uh, Ann does the financial management for our family. If I did, I think we'd both be in jail by now because I hate paying bills and keeping records, and Ann is very meticulous about it. She also has a phenomenal record of our thirty years together.

Interviewer: She's the historian?

Jim: And they're all catalogued neatly in albums where they can be seen, not stuck in drawers, which is what I would do, or a . . . And it's *wonderful* because friends will come from ten years ago, and we'll pull out an album and it will have pictures that they remember. It's very meaningful. And that's a talent that I don't have at all.

Ann: I think that there's several, there's several things that make our marriage very special, and I think strengthen almost any relationship. And one is – I think Jim has alluded to it before – respect for each other. We both respect what the other does, and we're committed to our marriage. And we give each other space when we need to have time alone, but then we love to be together! We just love to spend *time* being in each other's company. We *enjoy* each other. At least I enjoy being with *you*!

Jim: Definitely I enjoy being with you!

Interviewer: Yeah. Can you think of experiences over the years that have particularly bonded you?

Ann: Mmm . . . Oh, yes!

Jim: Working overseas–

Ann: Living in a tent for three months–

Jim: In the desert in Somalia.

Ann: That was a fairly bonding experience. And of course our two children have bonded us.

Jim: Oh yeah.

Interviewer: Now, did you, did you know before you got married how many kids you wanted to have?

Ann: We knew that we *wanted to* have children. We didn't talk numbers, except I remember somewhere thinking that maybe six would be nice.

Interviewer: Six!

Jim: I remember!

Ann: And then we thought maybe four, and then after we had two boys we decided that two was *just fine*. But that was a bonding experience – raising our two sons – going through being parents for them as young children, and the teenage years, which were not necessarily the happiest of times.

Jim: They were, uh, *challenging*.

Ann: And now our sons are old enough so that we treat each other as *equals*. All four of us are adults now, so when we get together, it's just a wonderful adult-to-adult relationship.

Narrator: Now complete the steps in your book.

Narrator: **Chapter 10, Love**
Page 135
Note taking: Taking advantage of rhetorical questions, Step 1

Narrator: Stop the tape after each beep and write your prediction.
One.

Lecturer: Why do you fall in love with *one* person but not *another* person?

Narrator: Two.

Lecturer: A lotta people might like a *ten*, but if you're a *five*, then who are you gonna end up getting married to?

Narrator: Three.

Lecturer: If she graduated from graduate school and he flunked outa kindergarten, do

you think that relationship is gonna last very long?

Narrator: Four.

Lecturer: You'd have the same age or about. Now, what's kinda the accepted age range?

Narrator: Five.

Lecturer: Now, what about the idea that opposites attract?

Narrator: Six.

Lecturer: You know that story of Romeo and Juliet?

Narrator: Now complete the steps in your book.

Narrator: **Chapter 10, Love**
Page 135
Note taking: Taking advantage of rhetorical questions, Step 2

Narrator: One.

Lecturer: Why do you fall in love with *one* person but not *another* person? Well, the sociobiology people, they would tend to say you fall in love – unconsciously – with somebody that's a good genetic match. Or something like that.

Narrator: Two.

Lecturer: A lotta people might like a *ten*, but if you're a *five*, then who are you gonna end up getting married to? Well, probably somebody closer to a five.

Narrator: Three.

Lecturer: If she graduated from graduate school and he flunked outa kindergarten, do you think that relationship is gonna last very long? Probably not.

Narrator: Four.
You'd have the same age or about. Now, what's kinda the accepted age range? Usually five to ten years.

Narrator: Five.

Lecturer: Now, what about the idea that opposites attract? You've probably heard that, that's kinda the *complementary* theory, or *complementarity*.

Narrator: Six.

Lecturer: You know that story of Romeo and Juliet? Uh, their families *hated* each other, and they said, "You stay away from him!" "You stay away from her!"

Narrator: Chapter 10, Love
Page 137
Outlining practice, Step 2

Lecturer: This seems to be one of the more difficult topics to discuss. Uh, what's this thing called love? It seems everybody has a different idea about *love*. Why do you fall in love with *one* person but not *another* person? Well, the sociobiology people, they would tend to say you fall in love – unconsciously – with somebody that's a good genetic match. Or something like that. "Boy, she'd produce nice kids, so I love her!" Now, sometimes, women like guys that are, uh, tall, muscular. Well, the sociobiologist would say that, well, they would produce a good, you know, gene pool. You know, that's why we like tall muscular types – you know, something like that. Now, even though you might *like* somebody – and you say, "Wow, is *she* beautiful" – well, it's like that movie *Ten*. You know, a lotta people might like a *ten*, but if you're a *five*, then who are you gonna end up getting married to? Well, probably somebody closer to a *five*. We tend to marry people that, that're like *we* are. We tend to really *like* people that're like we are. And that's *homogeneity*, or *similarity*. Some people call this the *matching hypothesis* – that we tend to be attracted to somebody that's like us. In fact, you're apt to *stay* married, *too*, if you marry somebody that's like you are.

Of course, the matching part is more than just *physical*. Uh, maybe you've seen a couple walking down the street and said, "Wow, what's *she* doing with *him*?" Maybe she's a ten and he's a three, or something, or the other way around. And what *that* is is that when you match up with someone, first you notice the physical package, but then you start adding in things like their *personality*, their job, their intelligence, maybe, and when you look at the total, you might decide that they're a good match

for you even if *physically* maybe they're *not*.

What else? Like, let's see, what'd be some things that . . . ? One'd be the same *educational* background. If she graduated from graduate school and he flunked outa kindergarten, do you think that's gonna last very long? Probably not. Like, for example, I recall one student in a four-year college – a long time ago – that she didn't go on to *graduate* school because she was afraid it would break up the marriage. And he'd just graduated from high school. She's graduated from college. And he kept bugging her about being a college graduate. "You're so smart! Why don't you do it!" Right? "Well, you're the college-educated one!" Y'know, that sorta thing. So, she didn't wanna have even *more* of a gap, so she actually stayed *down*, you might say, cuz he didn't wanna go *up*. Now that's kinda too bad. So, we tend to marry somebody that's similar in education. Often you *met* 'em in school.

What else should they be the same about? Uh, *interests*! You'd have about the same interests often. What else? Maybe the same *values*. OK. Same religion, maybe. Same race. Same age or *about*. Now, uh, what's kinda the accepted age range, that, uh . . . ? Usually five to ten years with exceptions, of course. But usually within five to ten years. What else would there be? Uh, socio-economic status, age, education, race, religion, values, interests, things like that.

Narrator: Now complete the steps in your book.

Narrator: Chapter 10, Love
Page 138
Outlining practice, Step 2

Lecturer: OK, so, generally the more similar you, similar you are, the more apt you are to stay married. And that really works. But you might say, "Well, *gee*, Bob! I'm a guy who flunked kindergarten and my wife has a graduate degree." Or, uh, "My mom has a degree and my dad never graduated from high school." Or, uh, what? Uh, I dunno. "He's *Catholic* and she's *Jewish*," or "She's twenty-three and he's forty-two," or whatever it might be. And, "Hey, they've been doin' *fine*!" That could be. But, as a *general* rule, the more *different* you are in these, it, it just increases your probability of getting a divorce.

Uh, we also tend to find people who have similar politics to what we have. If you're liberal, you'll tend to *marry* someone that's liberal. Or a conservative'll marry a conservative cuz you don't wanna marry someone who keeps telling you you're wrong! So, we also marry someone who sorta validates our ideas. We're kinda psychologically comfortable with those people. And, as I said, these marriages have a greater chance of lasting.

Now, what about the idea that opposites attract? You've probably heard that, that's kinda the *complementary* theory, or *complementarity*. I dunno why it is academics try to make big words outa little words. Instead of the difference theory, y'know, they say *complementary* theory or complementarity, or something like that. But anyway. Difference. Well, that can work for *magnets*. With people, difference is not, it doesn't work as well as similarity does, but it can be a factor. Uh, like if one person is *dominant*, are they better off with another dominant person, or are they better off with a person that's more submissive, that *likes* people telling 'em what to do? Probably a dominant person is more

apt to marry a submissive person. And maybe he or she likes the other person to be dominant and that works out *OK*. So, there *is* something to that. Probably two dominants don't work well, or maybe two submissives don't work well: "*Whaddyou* wanna do?" "I dunno, whatever. Whadda *you* wanna do?" "I dunno. Whatever *you* wanna do!" So, maybe, so that probably won't work too well. But, in general, the research that we have says that people that marry someone that's like they *are* tend to stay together.

One other factor that can bring a couple together is called the *Romeo and Juliet effect*. You know that story of Romeo and Juliet? You know, their families *hated* each other, and they said, "You stay away from him!" "You stay away from her!" So, what did Romeo and Juliet do? Yeah, they got married. So, the Romeo and Juliet theory says that the more *opposition* you face to a relationship, from parents or friends, or whoever, the more *attractive* that relationship *is* to you. The more people say, "Don't! You shouldn't!" the more you wanna do it. Pretty interesting, huh? And it turns out that these couples usually stay together, too.

So, those are some of the things that bring people together. And probably the most important thing to remember is the *similarity* idea – that we tend to be attracted to and happy with people who are like us.

Narrator: Now complete the steps in your book. This is the end of Chapter 10. This is the end of the audio program. Thanks for listening.

LECTURE QUIZZES AND ANSWERS

Lecture Quiz Answers

CHAPTER 1 Lecture Quiz Answers

1 Students should name two of the following: migraine headaches, high blood pressure, skin rashes, ulcers, heart disease.

2 It is the study of the connection between stress and illness or how the mind influences the functioning of the immune system.

3 He discovered that the immune system can be conditioned or taught to malfunction, which suggests that it can also be conditioned to get better.

4 Patients who choose to be in nursing homes tend to be healthier because they have some control over their lives; There appears to be a connection between health and feeling in control of one's situation.

5 They encourage them to practice relaxation techniques as a way to control certain medical conditions, such as headaches and sleeplessness.

CHAPTER 2 Lecture Quiz Answers

1 One or more arteries to the brain become blocked.

2 Men do. Women are protected by estrogen until menopause.

3 Family history, or heredity, is usually the explanation.

4 Obese people are more likely to develop diabetes and high blood pressure, which are both risk factors for cardiovascular disease.

5 Type A people are competitive, perfectionist, and easily angered. Type As, who frequently feel anger and hostility, are more at risk for cardiovascular disease.

CHAPTER 3 Lecture Quiz Answers

1 They often have suffered physical or sexual abuse; They turn to drugs to escape from the negative feelings they have about themselves.

2 It is important for the therapist to help the addict to experience feelings and for the therapist to accept these feeling without judging (i.e., reacting negatively toward) them.

3 Students should name two of the following: failing classes, acting out in school, not going to school.

4 Parents should not do a child's homework for him or her at the last minute, even if this means that the child ends up receiving a failing grade.

5 Adolescents are trying to understand who they are and to become more independent, but they still need their families as a source of nurturing and identity.

CHAPTER 4 Lecture Quiz Answers

1 Children in their early twenties are expected to become independent from their parents in all ways: financially, emotionally, and socially.

2 It is more difficult today for young people to become financially independent because of greater job competition and the rising cost of living.

3 They must be able to establish intimacy. This involves being willing and able to compromise, sacrifice, and negotiate.

4 Strain is created when two people are trying to build a marriage while at the same time they are still developing their own individual personalities.

5 Students should name two of the following reasons: less social pressure to marry young, greater desire to have the freedom to do other things, skepticism about marriage due to the high divorce rate.

CHAPTER 5 Lecture Quiz Answers

1 Binet based his intelligence test on the theory that intelligence increases with age: the older one gets, the smarter one gets.

2 A child's IQ score is calculated by dividing the mental age of the child by the child's actual age and then multiplying the answer by 100.

3 They are easier to administer, and they test both verbal skills and some performance skills, such as putting together puzzles.

4 They predict how well a person will do in school. They do not predict how well a person will do on the job or how successful a person will be in life.

5 They measure the kinds of intelligence more common among educated people of the middle and upper classes. They do not measure other kinds of intelligence, such as that needed to survive in the real world.

CHAPTER 6 Lecture Quiz Answers

1 He discovered that bright rats (i.e., good maze learners) had babies that were also bright and that dull rats (i.e., poor maze learners) had babies that were also dull.

2 They found that their IQ scores were very similar, which seemed to indicate that nature is an important factor in determining one's intelligence.

3 He found that the brains of rats that had been raised in an enriched environment were more developed than the brains of rats that had been raised in an impoverished environment.

4 According to Zajonc, the oldest child has a higher IQ because this child is brought up in an environment with a higher intellectual climate (i.e., average IQ) than his or her younger siblings. This shows that environment is an important factor in determining intelligence.

5 Students should name three of the following: increased TV watching, drug use, food, funding for schools, single parenting, two-career families, day care.

CHAPTER 7 Lecture Quiz Answers

1 She is surprised because we usually focus so much attention on the words we choose when we express things. Most of us think that our use of words is very important in communication.

2 Students should name three of the following: body language, posture, gestures, facial expressions, eye contact, tone of voice, touch.

3 In the United States direct eye contact is normal and appropriate, but in Japan there is less direct eye contact. In the United States *not* looking someone directly in the eye is disrespectful, but in Japan this is not true.

4 Depending on the nonverbal cues, such as tone of voice and the gestures and posture that accompany the word *maybe*, it can mean either "maybe yes" or "definitely no."

5 She recommends that we study, observe, and pay close attention to our own patterns of body language and the body language of the people around us.

CHAPTER 8 Lecture Quiz Answers

1 Sarcasm is a form of humor in which nonverbal cues make it clear that the speaker really believes the opposite of what he or she is saying. Sarcasm relates to the topic of the lecture because it proves that nonverbal cues can carry the real meaning of a message.

2 They adapt their position in some way: turning, moving away, putting books in front of them, or closing their jackets.

3 Students should name two of the following: the degree of intimacy between them, the social context, their gender relationship, their culture.

4 Students should name three of the following: affection, anger, playfulness, control, status.

5 People of the same sex holding hands in public.

CHAPTER 9 Lecture Quiz Answers

1 (1) A person who has a strong network of friends has a lower risk of committing suicide. (2) A person's family and friends can help watch over that person and keep him or her safe.

2 When we make friends with someone, we risk being rejected by them, which can be very painful.

3 Women like to talk to each other about their lives. Men feel more comfortable doing an activity with their male friends.

4 Men try to solve or fix the problem. Women just try to listen.

5 He was surprised because Anita Hill had told the witness that she was being sexually harassed by her boss and the witness had not given Ms. Hill any advice – she had simply listened to her. The senator could not understand this response.

CHAPTER 10 Lecture Quiz Answers

1 The sociobiologist would say that we are attracted to someone whom we unconsciously perceive as being a good genetic match in terms of his or her physical appearance and the kind of children he or she would produce.

2 The matching hypothesis states that we are attracted to people whom we see as being similar to us. Even though two people may not be equally attractive physically, they may have other similarities, such as common interests, level of education, etc.

3 Students should name five of the following: personality type, job, intelligence, level of education, interests, values, religion, race, age, socioeconomic status, political beliefs.

4 The lecturer says that a dominant person would probably get along better with a submissive person. If two submissive people lived together, they would have trouble deciding anything because they would each want the other person to decide everything.

5 As in the story of Romeo and Juliet, a couple will tend to feel more attracted to each other if there is opposition to their relationship from parents or friends.

CHAPTER 1 Lecture Quiz

Answer the following questions on Parts One and Two of the Chapter 1 lecture, *Stress and the Immune System*. Use only the lecture notes that you took on your own paper to help you. Answer each question as fully as possible. You will receive 2 points for each complete and correct answer and 1 point for each partially correct answer.

1 Name two health problems referred to in the lecture that can be psychosomatic disorders, that is, that can be caused by psychological problems.

2 What is psychoneuroimmunology?

3 What did Ader discover by accident while experimenting on rats and why was his discovery important?

4 Which group of elderly patients in nursing homes tends to be healthier and why?

5 What are more and more doctors encouraging their patients to practice and why?

Total score: _____/10

CHAPTER 2 Lecture Quiz

Answer the following questions on Parts One and Two of the Chapter 2 lecture, *Risk Factors in Cardiovascular Disease*. Use only the lecture notes that you took on your own paper to help you. Answer each question as fully as possible. You will receive 2 points for each complete and correct answer and 1 point for each partially correct answer.

1   What is happening when a person has a stroke?

2   Who has more cardiovascular disease, men or women? Why?

3   When a man in his thirties has a heart attack or stroke, what is the usual explanation?

4   What is the connection between obesity and cardiovascular disease?

5   What is the type A personality, and which part of it puts a person at increased risk for cardiovascular disease?

Total score: _____/10

CHAPTER 3 Lecture Quiz

Answer the following questions on Parts One and Two of the Chapter 3 lecture, *Common Problems of Adolescents in Mental Health Treatment.* Use only the lecture notes that you took on your own paper to help you. Answer each question as fully as possible. You will receive 2 points for each complete and correct answer and 1 point for each partially correct answer.

1 What type of abuse have many drug addicts suffered and why do they then turn to drugs or alcohol?

2 What is it important for the therapist to do in the early stages of drug addiction therapy?

3 Name two behaviors that a teacher might notice that could signal a child is having a problem at home.

4 What example does the lecturer give of a *clear set of rules* that a parent should establish with their children?

5 Why is adolescence such a difficult time, according to the lecturer?

Total score: _____/10

CHAPTER 4 Lecture Quiz

Answer the following questions on Parts One and Two of the Chapter 4 lecture, *Developmental Tasks of Early Adulthood*. Use only the lecture notes that you took on your own paper to help you. Answer each question as fully as possible. You will receive 2 points for each complete and correct answer and 1 point for each partially correct answer.

1   What is considered to be the ideal relationship for parents and children in Western cultures once the children become young adults?

2   Why are young people today living at home with their parents longer than young people did in the past?

3   According to Erikson, what do partners need to be able to do in order for a marriage to succeed?

4   According to the lecturer, what can create great stress or strain in a marriage?

5   Why are young people waiting longer to get married than in the past?

Total score: _____/10

CHAPTER 5 Lecture Quiz

Answer the following questions on Parts One and Two of the Chapter 5 lecture, *Intelligence Testing – An Introduction.* Use only the lecture notes that you took on your own paper to help you. Answer each question as fully as possible. You will receive 2 points for each complete and correct answer and 1 point for each partially correct answer.

1 What underlying theory did Binet use to construct his intelligence test?

2 What formula does the Stanford-Binet test use to calculate a child's IQ score?

3 In what two ways are the Wechsler scales an improvement over the Stanford-Binet?

4 What do IQ test scores predict and what do they not predict?

5 According to the lecturer, in what way are intelligence tests biased? Explain.

Total score: _____/10

CHAPTER 6 Lecture Quiz

Answer the following questions on Parts One and Two of the Chapter 6 lecture, *Intelligence –
Nature or Nurture?* Use only the lecture notes that you took on your own paper to help you.
Answer each question as fully as possible. You will receive 2 points for each complete and
correct answer and 1 point for each partially correct answer.

1 What did William Tryon discover when he bred rats in the 1940s?

2 What did researchers find when they studied the IQ scores of identical twins that had been
raised apart, and what did this tell researchers?

3 What did Hebbe discover when he examined the brains of rats raised in different
environments?

4 The oldest child almost always has a higher IQ than his or her siblings. According to
Zajonc, this gives support to the nurture side of the nurture/nature debate. Explain.

5 List three environmental factors mentioned at the end of the lecture that could influence
a child's intelligence.

Total score: _____/10

CHAPTER 7 Lecture Quiz

Answer the following questions on Parts One and Two of the Chapter 7 lecture, *Body Language Across Cultures*. Use only the lecture notes that you took on your own paper to help you. Answer each question as fully as possible. You will receive 2 points for each complete and correct answer and 1 point for each partially correct answer.

1 Why is the lecturer surprised that experts say, "Somewhere between 60 and 90 percent of everything we communicate is nonverbal?"

2 Name three things that people use to communicate nonverbally.

3 Explain how eye contact in the United States and in Japan is different.

4 Explain how the word *maybe* in Japanese, as an answer to a question asking for permission, can mean different things.

5 At the end of the lecture, what does the lecturer say is important to do and interesting, too?

Total score: _____/10

CHAPTER 8 Lecture Quiz

Answer the following questions on Parts One and Two of the Chapter 8 lecture, *Nonverbal Communication – The Hidden Dimension of Communication*. Use only the lecture notes that you took on your own paper to help you. Answer each question as fully as possible. You will receive 2 points for each complete and correct answer and 1 point for each partially correct answer.

1 What is sarcasm? How does it relate to the topic of the lecture?

2 How do people react when someone violates their personal space? Name two specific possibilities.

3 Name two factors that can influence the amount of space between two people who are communicating.

4 Name three things that touch can express.

5 Give an example from the lecture of touching behavior that is taboo in American culture.

Total score: _____/10

CHAPTER 9 Lecture Quiz

Answer the following questions on Parts One and Two of the Chapter 9 lecture, *Looking at Friendship*. Use only the lecture notes that you took on your own paper to help you. Answer each question as fully as possible. You will receive 2 points for each complete and correct answer and 1 point for each partially correct answer.

1 Give two reasons why a therapist wants to know about the social networks of a person who is suicidal.

2 What does the lecturer mean when he says that friendship can be a *risky business*?

3 Compare what usually happens when women get together with their friends to what happens when men get together.

4 How do men and women respond differently when their partners tell them about problems they are having?

5 Why was the senator questioning a female witness in the Clarence Thomas hearings so surprised?

Total score: _____/10

CHAPTER 10 Lecture Quiz

Answer the following questions on Parts One and Two of the Chapter 10 lecture, *Love – What's It All About?* Use only the lecture notes that you took on your own paper to help you. Answer each question as fully as possible. You will receive 2 points for each complete and correct answer and 1 point for each partially correct answer.

1 How would a sociobiologist explain the attraction that one individual might have for another?

2 How does the matching hypothesis explain the fact that sometimes a beautiful woman loves an unattractive man, or a handsome man loves an unattractive woman?

3 List five areas mentioned by the lecturer in which you might expect to find similarities between people who are attracted to each other.

4 According to the lecturer, sometimes it is better for people in a relationship to have differences. Explain how the example that he gives illustrates this.

5 Explain the Romeo and Juliet effect.

Total score: _____/10